In the Eye of the Hurricane is an
how a family in need can rise abo
solutions to the difficulties they fac▒. ▒▒▒▒er than be inhibited by the
lack of available services when their young son was diagnosed with
autism, Juli and Gordon designed a structured curriculum incorporating
direct instruction and best practices. The resulting changes have been
amazing. Ben was transformed from a child who was out of control to an
exceptional accelerated learner. I fully endorse the manuscript and think
it will provide other parents who have children with disabilities with hope
and inspiration.

Dr. Mark T. Harvey, BCBA, PhD
Dept. of Special Education, Vanderbilt University

****

I have had the opportunity to review the Liske's programming, see
videos of their early sessions, and observe Juli doing therapy with Ben.
It was difficult to believe she had no formal training in ABA or autism.
The early videos documented Ben's autism. He was nonverbal, had
difficulty attending to and interacting with his parents, and engaged in
self-stimulating behaviors. When I observed Ben in 2004, he enjoyed
interaction with his parents, was able to speak in full sentences, and could
read fluently. The Liskes were able to achieve a miraculous outcome for
their child!

Juli is an inspiration to parents everywhere. She is proof that parents
can help their children make tremendous gains, even when professionals
are unavailable. I have had the privilege of reading her book. I feel
that parents of children with autism need a book like this to encourage
them. They need to see that they can help their children by educating
themselves. This book would also be beneficial to professionals. Parents
are a child's best resource. Professionals providing services to families
with autistic children need to recognize the importance of the parents' role
in their child's success. One day I hope to be able to recommend Juli's
book to all the families to whom I provide services.

Lisa Maurer Ellzy, BSSW, MA

****

In the Eye of the Hurricane

A riveting read that plunges deep into one family's world of autism. Author Juli Liske spins a real life but atypical autism tale of two rural, working-class parents who confront discouraging, deeply entrenched and disturbing manifestations of the disorder with sheer grit and admirably relentless determination. This is not a book about a wealthy family with a plethora of money, personnel, and resources. And, therein lies, in part, the inspiration and encouragement this book gifts the reader. Another gift for readers is learning how the Liske family burrowed in and created an innovative home-spun intervention team, which is also a lesson in creativity and ingenuity. What results is the culling of an extraordinary little boy and a mother's journey from despair into the genuine realization of autism's special blessings. A worthy addition to anyone's library!

Leisa A. Hammett, mother, advocate, author of forthcoming book: *The Journey with Grace: a mother's reflections of raising a child with autism*

****

*Juli Liske's **In the Eye of the Hurricane** is a profoundly beautiful and moving book. To read it is to share in the journey of the Liske family, not just from rural Eastern Kentucky to Middle Tennessee, but also in their journey from brokenness to healing, from helplessness to empowerment, and from despair to hope. There is a very difficult struggle that parents of children on the autism spectrum come to know. That is, the struggle between the desire to do anything, everything that you possibly can for your child with autism to help ease his way and lessen his challenges, and on the other hand, the innate knowledge a parent has that despite what the world would have you believe, your child is perfect just as he is. Add in the challenges of keeping expectations as high as possible, and it's little wonder many families lose hope, give up the fight, and accept the status quo.*

***In the Eye of the Hurricane** is the story of a family calling on their inner reserve of faith to embrace that struggle and use it as a path to a richer life for themselves, and particularly for their son Ben. This story of how the Liske's crafted a program for Ben where no program existed,* *and are continuing to learn to challenge him in the ways he needs to bring out the unique, wonderful person that he will become, is a story that will inspire and challenge ALL of us to become better parents to our own children.*

John Shouse, Parent
2nd Vice Chair, Autism Society of America
Past President, Autism Society of Middle Tennessee

****

As I read this book, I was impacted on several levels. First, as a parent, my little boy was recently diagnosed with autism. Throughout the book, I found myself crying and smiling at the same time because of the realness to the experiences Juli shares. The similarities of our journeys are striking. From the frustration in dealing with medical professionals to the all consuming fear of facing such a difficult diagnosis, Juli has put words to the wide range of emotions experienced by myself and so many others.

On another level, as a professional in the field of developmental disabilities, I found Juli's writing to be reader friendly as well as responsible and written with integrity. She does not claim to have a cure for autism but is sharing a treatment method that has been effective with her son. She and her family demonstrate what commitment and hard work can achieve.

Lastly, as a Christian, I found myself relying on God and His Word for comfort and strength, specifically using many of the same passages Juli shares in her book.

In the Eye of the Hurricane *is a useful resource for any parent at any stage of this journey and for any professional seeking better understanding of a parent's perspective - Juli offers guidance and support for both parents and professionals. I am inspired by her determination, creativity, and commitment.*

Kimberly Dean, MA in Clinical Psychology
Director of Staff Development and Training, Division of Mental Retardation Services.

EYE OF THE HURRICANE

To Terri —
Best of luck with
the kids!
Juli C. Liske

In the Eye of the
HURRICANE

By Juli C. Liske

www.spiritbuilding.com for more tracts and study helps

SPIRITBUILDING PUBLISHING
15591 N. State Rd. 9, Summitville, Indiana, 46070
Spiritual "equipment" for winning the contest of life.

COVER : Photography on front and back cover by Jen Wood

Disclaimer

The author of this book is not a physician and the ideas and suggestions in this book are not intended as a substitute for the individualized advice and care of a licensed health professional. The author and publisher assume no liability arising directly or indirectly from the use of this book or any of the treatments mentioned in it. The statements made by the author in regard to any treatment regimens represent only the personal views and opinions of the author, and do not constitute a recommendation of any treatments by the publisher.

Note from the author:

The names and identifying details of persons in this book who could possibly be construed as being portrayed in a negative light have been changed to protect their right to privacy.

C O N T E N T S

To Papa

(known to thousands of children as

"The real Santa")

Who has made the world a better place by making a

difference in the lives of children—one child at a time.

To everything there is a season,
A time for every purpose under heaven:
A time to be born, and a time to die;
A time to plant, and a time to pluck what is planted;
A time to kill, and a time to heal;
A time to break down, and a time to build up;
A time to weep, and a time to laugh;
A time to mourn, and a time to dance;
A time to cast away stones, and a time to gather stones;
A time to embrace, and a time to refrain from embracing;
A time to gain, and a time to lose;
A time to keep, and a time to throw away;
A time to tear, and a time to sew;
A time to keep silence, and a time to speak;
A time to love, and a time to hate;
A time of war, and a time of peace.

Ecclesiastes 3:1-9 NKJV

Prologue

"We are hard pressed on every side, yet not crushed; we are perplexed, but not in despair; persecuted, but not forsaken; struck down, but not destroyed...."

2 Corinthians 4:8-9

"Maamaaa! Where are yooouu?!"

I could hear the sound of Ben's little feet as he bounced up the stairs. The rattle of paper could be heard as Ben arrived outside my bathroom door where I lay relaxing in a bubble bath.

Knock, knock.

"Who is it?" I asked, a smile forming around my lips.

The locked doorknob turned side to side. "It's me, Benjamin. Open the door, please."

"Mama is taking a bath, Baby-Love. But I'm almost finished. Can you wait just a minute?"

An impatient sigh.

Silence.

Then, his voice full of hope, "Are you done yet, Mama?"

I smiled to myself. Four-year-old Ben could consistently be relied upon to need me, desperately, as soon as I got into the bathtub each evening.

I grabbed my bathrobe, wrapped it around myself and unlocked the door. Ben's dancing storm blue eyes looked up into mine and an infectious grin burst across his beautiful face.

As I stood there cold and dripping, my heart was filled with love and the deepest gratitude to God as I beheld the face of this little angel.

He was so perfect, so handsome, so healthy and robust....

"Look, Mama, read it!" he exclaimed, holding up the paper he had made on the computer.

Ben smiled proudly as he waited for the praise he was sure would ensue. "Oh! That is so wonderful, Baby! You are so smart! I love you..." I kissed him on top of the head, breathing in his fresh clean scent.

Ben cocked his head to one side and smiled coyly, "I love you too, Mama..." He hugged me tightly around the legs before grabbing his paper and galloping off happily down the hall to show his masterpiece to his sister.

In his blue snowflake pajamas and house slippers he was beginning to look more and more like a little boy than a baby now. He was tall and well-built. He often reminded me of one of those handsome little boys you might see in a boy's choir with his rosy cheeks, perfect full lips, and neatly cropped sandy hair.

"Look! Sarah..."

Standing there watching him that night was such bittersweet victory. The scene was one that was so commonplace and ordinary...so normal....

This child who was once silent...now spoke.

Who was once violent...now loving.

Who was unreachable...now reaching out.

Whose future on this planet seemed forever lost...now restored.

We had weathered the storm...and survived. We were stronger now... much stronger.

We were living proof that the testing of one's faith produces patience.

The fear, grief, and hopelessness that had ruled our lives a little over two years before seemed now like a terrible nightmare that was fading with the light of the dawn.

And what a nightmare it had been....

PART I
The Gathering of the Clouds

Gordon getting the big welcome from
Dylan and Sarah on wedding day.

"Behold, children are a heritage from the Lord,
The fruit of the womb is His reward."
Psalm 127:3 NKJV

1

May 2, 2000

After a difficult pregnancy and a complicated delivery, my husband and I gazed breathlessly at the tiny form that lay lifeless and silent on my abdomen.

Dr. Priddle and his nurse stared anxiously as well before the doctor grabbed the tiny feet in one hand and slapped them once...twice...three times...the tiny arms gave a jerk!!!

Silence.

The doctor slapped the tiny feet once more.

Then, finally, the smallest whimper could be heard...

Benjamin began to move his head from side to side as if he were reluctantly waking from a deep sleep. "Waa..." he whimpered again.

"That cry ain't loud enough to suit me just yet, Boy!" Dr. Priddle exclaimed as he whisked him from my abdomen into the heated bassinet where he and his nurse proceeded to rub him down vigorously, check his oxygen saturation, and further examine him.

We could see the concerned expressions of the doctor and nurse begin to relax as we finally heard a hearty "WAAA! WAAAA!!!"

At the time of this printing, there is no known, specific cause of autism. Current research suggests there is a genetic correlation — although no single gene has been directly linked to autism.

Dr. Priddle smiled and held up a newly "pinked up" version of the frighteningly bluish baby he had taken from me a moment before. "Daddy, take a picture of your beautiful baby boy!"

Late that evening, I sat propped up in my hospital bed with Gordon peering over my shoulder curiously watching Benjamin's every blink and grimace.

That night as Ben studied my face, I whispered to Gordon, "You know, it's a scary thing to look into those little eyes and realize that they depend on you for everything. God has put us to the task of being everything to this tiny person."

Ben continued to look directly into my eyes as I spoke, "He looks at us as if he knows that or something. Do you know what I mean? And I always thought newborns couldn't see well, but look. He even looks like he is listening to what I am saying."

Ben's eyes shifted back and forth from my face to Gordon's as we reveled in the magical moment that all new parents experience whether it is their first child or their tenth.

****

After seven weeks of blissful motherhood, I reluctantly returned to my job as a dental hygienist. The only consolation being that Gordon had ninety days of paternity leave which he arranged to begin the day I returned to work.

Our close-knit office consisted of four females with the dentist, Jennifer, being my age and delivering her first child only nine days after Ben's birth.

We were equally reluctant to leave our babies and spent the work days telling baby stories and comparing diaper brands.

The separation was eased as much as it could be, with my mother's-guilt placated only by the fact that Jennifer and I had agreed to no longer work on Fridays and that Benjamin was safely nestled in Daddy's arms for the time being.

During Gordon's paternity leave, we searched for the perfect person to keep our baby. After endless interviews, we finally settled on a woman who lived one block from my office in order for me to go over during lunch to feed Ben.

Charlotte seemed to adore Ben and he seemed to love her. At five months old, he was just beginning to roll over and was becoming increasingly gregarious and engaging. However, something still bothered me about leaving Ben.

I had noticed in the past few weeks that Ben was frequently stiffening his body when I held him and would often attempt to throw himself backward out of my arms. He seemed to be crying excessively for no apparent reason. We could find nothing to justify such crying fits. He was too old to be developing colic. Gordon and I tried to reason that maybe he was beginning to get teeth, maybe he had a headache, maybe he was just becoming spoiled....

As difficult as Ben was becoming for Gordon or myself to manage for longer and more frequent periods of time, I began to worry about leaving him with anyone. After all, no one loves a child more and can tolerate challenging behavior more than his own parents, right? What if, one day, Charlotte just had enough and began abusing or neglecting him? Dare we take that risk? After four weeks, we decided to let Charlotte go.

Gordon and I discussed my quitting work and came to the conclusion that we simply could not get by without my income no matter how we tried to budget. Finally, we were able to adjust both our work schedules so that one of us could always be home with the baby. I worked during the day and Gordon worked during the evening and on Fridays and Saturdays.

At Benjamin's six-month checkup, our family physician, Dr. Charles, could find nothing to justify such turbulent behavior and dismissed it as "his disposition." Benjamin, by all appearances, was a healthy boy except for a chronically itchy nose. He was constantly pawing at his nose, which was often runny, but had no fever or other signs of an actual "cold." We assumed this must be the precursor to a future allergy problem.

We visited an allergist who was quick to inform us that babies this small did not have "real" allergies. Just to be safe, Gordon and I opted to get rid of the family cat anyway.

By six months, Ben had reached the 100th percentile in height and the 95th percentile in weight. He was in all respects a beautiful baby with thick, dark eyebrows and eyelashes that perfectly offset his unusual deep-navy eyes. Even a few of the burly macho men of our rural Kentucky town often surprisingly commented, "He's so...so...Well...he's just...a purdy li'l guy."

Much of the time, Ben was a happy child, smiling and seeking out others to interact with. More and more frequently, however, the raging storms were beginning to roll in...

2

"The wind blows where it wishes, and you hear the sound of it, but cannot tell where it comes from and where it goes...." John 3:8 NKJV

...in retrospect, I still cannot quite put my finger on when the unusual behavior shifted from the occasional unwarranted temper tantrum to the more frequent episodes that ultimately came to dominate every moment of our family life.

At around seven months, Ben began to make what we thought at the time were cute funny faces in which he would either wrinkle up his nose and squint at us or tuck his chin down to his chest, furrow his brow, and look at us as though he were peering over bifocals.

Autism is defined as a lifelong, neurobiological condition that significantly affects how a person perceives the world, interacts with other people, and communicates.

The later expression was somewhat frightening looking to me in that it reminded me of the way a demon-possessed individual is often portrayed in the movies. Interestingly, we noticed that Ben only made these faces while he was lying on his back looking toward the overhead lights. We took several photographs of Mr. Funny Face, not realizing that these expressions were a shadow of the storm to come.

At eight months, Ben began to crawl. One sunny Saturday morning in December, Ben had crawled to the edge of our large living room area rug and was closely inspecting a very small section of the hardwood flooring where the boards were further apart than the rest. He studied it for at least five minutes before crawling away. I had watched this with much curiosity only to realize that he wasn't crawling away but rather making his way around to re-examine this same crevice, but from a different angle! How odd!

When Gordon came home I described this scenario to him and he was as much at a loss as I had been. Over the next few months, we were to watch

In the realm of developmental milestones, Benjamin was right on schedule. With so many years between the time my two older children, Dylan and Sarah, were small and Benjamin's birth, it was often fuzzy in my mind exactly what he should be doing and when without consulting child development books and comparing notes with Jennifer at work on the progress of her daughter Lauren. Up until their first birthdays, other than the typical height and weight differences between boys and girls, Ben and Lauren were a close match developmentally. But in the few months leading up to his first birthday, Ben began to withdraw socially.

The once smiling, rosy-cheeked baby began to avoid eye contact at all costs. Those intense, formerly searching, deep-blue eyes could now only be captured for a fleeting moment. Close friends from church whom Ben had endlessly cooed and giggled with could no longer gain his attention.

I remember one particular Sunday morning in February 2001. As we were making our way out the front door of the church building, I stopped to greet brother Tol, our preacher. He, in his customary way, took Ben's little hand in his and patted it saying, "Bye-bye Benjamin! Tell me bye!"

Ben, who in months past would have kicked his legs and giggled with excitement at seeing brother Tol smile and speak to him, stared blankly over his head at the clock as if no one had even spoken.

Brother Tol attempted his social overture again only to be met by the same response. Embarrassed, all I could do was shake my head sheepishly, "He sure seems worried about that clock up there."

In an attempt to humor Tol and mollify myself I said, "He must be trying to tell you that you preached too long!"

****

On Ben's first birthday, we had fifteen guests which included the three girls from the office with their children and two couples from church.

The party theme was Sesame Street's "Elmo," with which Ben had in recent months become almost obsessed. During the party, we had an "Elmo" tape playing in the VCR in hopes of preventing Ben from having one of his frequent unprovoked fits and making a scene in front of his guests.

Ben was entirely oblivious to the fact that three babies and four children were crawling and running all over the same room.

Several times during the party people would make comments like, "Wow! I can't believe how intense Ben is!"

"He must really love 'Elmo'!"

"It's almost as if no one is here!"

Frustrated, I finally turned off the tape hoping Ben might notice his company only to find him crawling over to the offending floor crevice which I had since covered with the rug. Unperturbed, he flipped up the corner of the rug and began his ritualistic examination.

When it was time to open gifts, Ben was no more interested than he had been in his guests. Ben's older sister, Sarah, ended up doing most of the opening for him all the while trying to catch his attention with one of the many gifts that had been so thoughtfully chosen for him by our friends. Even the piles of colorful paper and bows were not worthy of a glance.

Ben instead chose to complacently sit looking at an old lift-the-flap board book and seemed mostly fascinated with the actual process of lifting the flap than with what was hidden underneath.

The other babies were walking and crawling about babbling, pointing, and vying for possession of the noisiest toys. Despite the fact that the entire floor was completely covered with new toys and books, Benjamin continued to sit quietly looking at his book until finally the last gift was opened.

Autism is a spectrum disorder. Although autism is defined by a certain set of behaviors, individuals can exhibit any combination of the behaviors in any degree of severity.

It was brother Tol who lifted the final gift from the floor and tore back the paper to reveal an ordinary kitchen wall clock.

"Look, Ben! A clock!"

I had picked up the clock at Wal-Mart almost as an afterthought, thinking Ben might enjoy having it hung in his bedroom. Ben looked up and actually smiled, dropped his book and crawled over to brother Tol and sat admiring his new clock. The tiny ticking second hand seemed to be the focus of his fascination.

The highlight of the party turned out to be the traditional first birthday cake demolition. Gordon placed Ben on the table in front of his bright red cake shaped like Elmo's face. Ben smiled and began to gingerly swipe at the cake with one tiny finger before ultimately destroying the cake with both hands and feet. I was relieved that at least one aspect of Ben's party went as planned, and everyone enjoyed watching the icing-coated birthday boy enjoy himself.

Later on, the guests began to leave one by one, and Gordon carefully carried a happy, cake-encrusted Benjamin to the bathtub while I crawled about the living room floor gathering paper, bows, and toys.

Jennifer had become engaged in conversation with our preacher's wife, Dana. Jennifer and her husband were proudly demonstrating how Lauren could show how old she was going to be next week.

"Lauren, how old are you gonna be?"

Lauren grinned and held up one tiny, chubby finger.

As I listened to their conversation, it was then that I realized that Ben had yet to demonstrate that he had ever understood anything that was said to him by gesturing, speaking, or otherwise. Nor had I ever seen him point to indicate that he wanted something in the way all three of the other same-aged babies at the party had done. This realization made my heart pound in my chest.

As I stuffed the remainder of the torn wrapping paper into the trash bag, I began to feel nauseous. Why must Jennifer and I always compare our babies anyway? Perhaps Ben just doesn't have anything to say yet. Maybe he had a hearing problem? You know, he was really bad for getting that hard corky wax build-up in his ears from time to time that had to be removed by the doctor. Maybe I'm not spending as much time with him trying to stimulate his language development as I should....

****

Benjamin had taken his first steps alone the day before his first birthday and within a few weeks, had broken into a full-fledged run.

He had begun to say a word or two from time to time, and Gordon and I had thought we had heard "Dada" once or twice. We knew for sure he had said "Ball," "Stop," and "Bird" but didn't realize until much later that as he would gain a new word here and there that he seemed to lose other words he had used in the past and that we never heard them again.

Gordon and I both made a point to take Ben around the house and yard pointing out objects. "Look! See the tree! Say tree!"

No response.

"See sky! Say sky!"

I couldn't get Ben to look at anything I pointed to without physically turning his head, much less get him to say anything.

When I wasn't trying to hold him to show him something, Ben was in constant motion. Instead of playing with toys, Ben would simply run back and forth across the lawn, tracking the dogwood tree with his eyes as he ran past.

Back and forth. Back and forth.

What was he doing?

Was the fascination with the tree or the running? I had never seen another child behave in this manner.

I would attempt to take him back inside only to be met with the fiercest of tantrums. When I tried to pick him up, he would arch his back violently and then grow completely limp. If I managed to lift him anyway, he would buck back and forth wildly in an attempt to be put down. Often he would rare back and slam his head so hard into my chest that it knocked the wind out of me. I was determined that this incredibly stubborn child *was not* going to call the shots around this house.

I would haul him inside, arms and legs flailing and kicking. I was sure Ben's incessant shrieking could be heard from blocks away. When we finally managed to get inside the house, Ben would lie on the floor screaming for three or four minutes before getting up and proceeding to run up and down the hallway.

Back and forth.

Back and forth...tracking the doorways with his eyes as he went....

3

"Every good gift and perfect gift is from above, and comes down from the Father of lights...." James 1:17 NKJV

Spring turned to summer and summer to fall.

Gordon had a long summer with Benjamin to tend during the day and Dylan and Sarah underfoot asking to go places and having friends in and out. They kept the house abuzz with the typical pre-adolescent bickering and fighting while Ben roared through our tiny house like a Tasmanian devil.

The start of school came as a welcome relief that year to Gordon especially. Gordon had always been a considerably patient man and took great pains to be an attentive and loving father. This particular summer, however, was stressful for us all.

When Gordon came into my life, I knew he had to be a gift straight from God. As step-father to Dylan and Sarah, Gordon took the job seriously and I couldn't have asked for more. He was kind and nurturing, yet consistent and firm in his parenting. Now I was overjoyed that Gordon had been willing to cut back his hours at work and had embraced the opportunity to take such an active role in the rearing of his first and only child.

What autism is not: a mental illness or the result of poor parenting

I had married at the tender age of eighteen and chosen to start a family right away. After 6½ years of heartache and two children, we divorced and I moved back to my hometown in Eastern Kentucky with four-year-old Dylan and three-year-old Sarah. I was able to purchase a small house and busied myself trying to make life stable for my children.

As a single mom struggling to get on my feet with two young children, I knew the chances of meeting a man that I loved, that loved me, that loved my kids, and my kids loved him were next to impossible.

Aside from being so consumed with caring for the emotional needs of my post-divorce children, working full-time, and trying to make ends meet, who had time to think of romance?

Gordon was a tall, well-built man with broad shoulders, strikingly handsome features, and beautiful silver wing-tipped hair. He had a deep, rumbling, gentle voice and a very distinct hearty laugh that made all in earshot feel happy.

Originally from Michigan and from 100% German stock, we were an unlikely but perfect match. Gordon was twelve years my senior and although the ultimate uncle, had never been blessed with the opportunity to have children of his own.

We both knew right away we were destined to marry. The next June, we were united in marriage in a small formal outdoor ceremony, with Dylan as ring-bearer and Sarah as flower girl. After saying our vows to one another, Gordon knelt down and said his own vows to each of the children. We were not only united as man and wife, but as a family.

****

Family life was blissful and I found myself yearning to bear a child for the man who was such a natural father. Gordon insisted that he was perfectly content with Dylan and Sarah and that they fulfilled his fatherly instinct in every way. He did not think it right to expect me to bear a third child simply because he did not have a biological child of his own.

After much discussion, I was finally able to convince him that I didn't feel obligated, but that I actually wanted to have another child. I found myself daydreaming about what a child of ours would look and be like.

Month after month passed and I still was not pregnant. After two years, Gordon and I both went through several batteries of fertility testing only to know no more than we had before. All we could do was wait.

Month after month my pregnancy tests turned out negative, and I cried inconsolably. Gordon had turned forty, and I felt he would never experience the joy of seeing his own child born.

Finally, after losing all hope, it happened. One morning in September, Pam, our dental assistant, greeted me at the door with the pregnancy test she insisted I take every month. I half-heartedly went into the bathroom, complaining that I was wasting my time and not wanting to get my hopes up again only to have them shot down. I closed the door, did my duty, and left the test in the bathroom.

A moment later I heard Pam screaming, "Come here!! Everybody! Come here!! It's positive!!!"

I walked back toward the bathroom thinking "What a cruel joke! That's not even funny!"

Pam was standing in the back doorway with the test turned toward the morning light, "Look! See, there's a line! I'm not kidding! Really!"

Pam, a notorious prankster, was actually telling the truth.

I couldn't believe my eyes.

Hesitant to believe, "Well, it is just a cheap generic test. Maybe I better run up and see Dr. Charles before I get too excited."

Dr. Charles' nurse, Gail, anxiously whisked me back to collect a blood sample and shuttled me back out the door so I could get back down to the office to seat my first patient of the morning.

Thirty minutes later, the phone rang. Gail and the entire staff were on the other end on speaker phone cheering, "Congratulations!!"

I was euphoric. Our secretary, Michelle, gift wrapped the original dollar store test for me to take home to Gordon.

Puzzled to be handed a gift in the middle of September, I could see Gordon frantically scanning his memory banks to figure out if he had forgotten a special day.

"No reason...just felt like it. Go ahead, open it."

After removing the test from the box, Gordon stared at the little stick for a few seconds before it finally registered, "You're pregnant?"

I nodded my head as he leapt to his feet and hugged me tightly. The children, not knowing what all the commotion was about, happily joined in the celebratory hugging.

****

True to form, Gordon was the perfect doting husband throughout the pregnancy and was everything I knew he would be during and after Ben's birth. By the end of the pregnancy, we knew this would be our only child due to the extent of complications I had experienced.

Being home during the day with a baby was a major adjustment for a man who had been in the workforce all his life, but Gordon gracefully accepted the challenge, realizing this would be his one and only opportunity to experience the first precious years of child-rearing.

I first felt reluctant to relinquish the role I had so enjoyed when Dylan and Sarah had been small, but soon came to realize the value of a husband and father who truly *wanted* to be present to witness all the milestones of his child. I also realized that with this arrangement, Benjamin would have equal time with each parent individually as well as collectively.

I learned to appreciate the distinctively different style of parenting that a man has to offer a child. Hard as it is to accept, wrinkled, mismatched clothes on a baby is not the worst thing that ever happened...it will not cause lasting harm.

Now, fifteen months later, Gordon was having a difficult time knowing exactly what to do with Benjamin.

One evening after all the children were in bed, I hesitantly asked, "Have you been reading to Ben every day and making a point to talk with him throughout the day? He's just not picking up words the way he ought to."

Somewhat on the defensive, Gordon answered, "Yes, I've been making a point to do those things just like you told me I should. Maybe he's just not going to be as smart as Dylan and Sarah. I know I have a lot of common sense, but I'm not the most book smart guy."

Some children with autism demonstrate a delay early in infancy, while others appear to develop typically until the age of 18-30 months, when parents may notice delays or regression in language, play, or social interaction.

Instantly, I felt a pang of remorse for what I had said. Yet I knew something was not right. I found myself increasingly avoiding play dates with Jennifer and Lauren for fear of seeing more missing in Ben than I wanted to see. More and more, I found myself making excuses for Ben's outlandish public displays of anger and for his lack of interest in others.

"He didn't get his nap."

"He must be teething again."

"Maybe he's getting another ear infection."

My heart went out to Gordon, knowing he must in some way feel he was inferior to my former husband, and I felt at a loss to make him see nothing could be further from the truth!

I walked to the back bedroom to retrieve Dylan's baby book to show Gordon the lists of words that Dylan could say at different points in his first three years. I knew the differences were huge, but actually comparing the baby books of each of my sons in black and white made the contrast become increasingly and frighteningly real.

I tried to reason as gently as possible that all children have different strengths and weaknesses that are all their own. But there came a time when things begin to look more and more like something other than mere differences.

Benjamin was not only developing socially and verbally more slowly than Dylan and Sarah, but also more slowly than Lauren and all the other babies at church. In fact, socially and verbally, Ben's development was practically non-existent.

The look of hurt in Gordon's eyes was more than I could bear. Selfishly, I began to sob. Gordon held me in his arms and tried to reassure me, even though he himself was not entirely certain of what the future might hold.

Late as it was, I heard a small voice call out from the bedroom, "Mom... Mom..."

I walked back to Dylan's room and found him peeking out his door, "Mom, what's wrong with Benjamin? Does he have a brain tumor or something?"

Realizing he had overheard our conversation, I held back the tears and tried to reassure him, "No, Baby, he's just not talking as much as we think he should. It'll be all right."

Dylan considered what I had said, "Gosh, I hope so. Good night, Mom. Give Ben a kiss for me."

Ben at 10 months old.

4

"The secret things belong to the Lord our God...."
Deuteronomy 29:29 NKJV

September and October of 2001 were busy months for our family, as all of us worked together to try to reach Benjamin. We voiced our concerns to Dr. Charles at Ben's routine checkup. Dr. Charles seemed to think the delays still appeared to fall within a normal, although late parameter.

Gordon and I spent hours in bookstores and educational stores examining different toys and materials with which to further stimulate Ben.

We also spent hundreds and hundreds of dollars that we could not afford to part with, but did so willingly in our futile efforts to make a difference. Somehow, I think we both thought subconsciously that the more we bought, the more we could fix what seemed to be wrong with our little boy. Maybe it would just disappear...whatever "it" was.

One ray of hope came when we found Benjamin taking an interest in the numerous alphabet and number puzzles we had purchased. He became quite adept at assembling each one but was more interested in taking the pieces out of the forms and meticulously lining them up across the floor. This soon became a daily ritual that could last for hours at a time.

At first, I was relieved that we had finally been able to pique his interest in something other than running back and forth down the hallway and was also pleased to discover an outward demonstration of intellect. In fact, in this respect, Benjamin soon proved to be developmentally ahead of schedule.

Other interesting behaviors also emerged. Ben began to walk about the house on his tiptoes, occasionally bouncing as he went. Gordon and I just considered it a passing phase and called him "Twinkle Toes." The toe-walking would persist for a few days and then cease for a week or so before it would start again.

Mealtimes were quickly becoming a major issue with Ben. He had readily accepted his pureed baby foods at five and six months. Later, he had also accepted some table foods, but these were very limited. Attempts to introduce any finger foods besides Cheerios or even baby foods that were slightly thick were met with an up-turned nose and often even gagging and vomiting at the mere sight of them. Benjamin seemed to have developed a sudden aversion to texture. This struck me as odd since just four short months before, he had happily wallowed in his birthday cake and seemed to thoroughly enjoy every moment of doing so. Now, just the sight of a single raisin on his highchair tray or even the prospect of actually having to touch play dough was repulsive to him!

A sippy cup was also met with stubborn rejection. I bought every type on the market, all to no avail. Ben refused to drink juice of any kind and resisted even transitioning from breast milk to cow's milk. The total time to make the complete transition from breast to bottle and finally to a cup (only with a straw, all sippy cups were out of the question) took over nine months.

Benjamin had always enjoyed music, as most babies and toddlers do. He seemed to look forward to Bible class, where the teacher spent at least half of the class time singing familiar children's Bible songs and teaching the toddlers the accompanying hand motions. Ben quickly learned all of the hand motions and would use them at the appropriate times during the songs. Curiously, however, Ben never once even attempted to sing the words like the other toddlers were learning to do.

Many children with autism are hypersensitive or hyposensitive to sight, sound, touch, smell, or taste. Any combination of sensory issues may be present, with multiple hypersensitivities and hyposensitivities often present within the same child.

Since he had become so difficult to feed as of late, I would often sing the same songs while I fed him in order to distract him. For several months it worked like a charm. As I would sing "This Little Light of Mine," Ben would smile and do his hand motions, and I would slip a bite in his mouth here and there.

Then, one day as I began singing "Deep and Wide" and started to feed him his lunch, Ben started screaming. Startled, I immediately stopped singing and he immediately stopped screaming. Every time I opened my mouth to sing, Ben would start screaming. At first I took it personally and thought Ben had finally grown sick of my singing. But when Gordon came home that evening, I asked him to try to feed Ben and sing.

Gordon began singing and Ben began screaming. We were completely baffled. Perhaps, we reasoned, Ben had grown wise to our plan of distraction in order to get him to eat? Perhaps he had decided if he didn't allow himself to be distracted, we wouldn't be able to slip in those strained green beans anymore.

This theory, however, was shot down when Gordon tried to sing to Ben during bath time that evening. Ben would scream angrily and continue to scream until the offending singer stopped singing.

This strange behavior persisted until finally, on Sunday morning, I thought it might be wise to sit in on Ben's Bible class to see what would happen when his teacher, Janet, started to sing. Ben had grown quite fond of Janet during the few months since she had started teaching his class and would beam whenever she spoke to him. This day seemed to be no different. I told Janet that Ben hadn't been behaving very well and that I thought I ought to sit in just in case.

Ben sat in his little seat with his eyes on Janet as if he just couldn't wait for her to start singing. I sat quietly behind Ben, ready to intervene when the fit began. Janet said, "Okay! Let's sing 'I Like to Come to Class.'"

"I like to come to class...I like to come to class...with all the other boys and girls, I like to come to class..."

Benjamin sat beaming at Janet and clapping his hands in time to the song. Relieved but puzzled, I thought maybe it had been just a fleeting phase.

Janet began the next song, "Zacchaeus was a wee little man and a wee little man was he.... He climbed up in the sycamore tree for the Lord he wanted to see...."

The children all sang happily and followed along with their hand motions. Ben smiled and kept perfect time with his hands.

I decided to join in, "...and as the Savior passed him by, he looked up...."

Ben angrily whipped around in his seat toward me, both hands furiously beating the air, "AHHHHH!! AHHHH!!"

I jumped back quickly to avoid being struck and reached out and grabbed the tiny flying fists. The teacher and all the children stopped their singing and looked at us as if searching for an explanation for this strange outburst.

Embarrassed and confused, I looked at Janet and blurted, "I just don't get it! It's as if he has suddenly decided that no one else is allowed to sing anything at anytime without him throwing a fit. But it's okay if you sing! It makes no sense."

Janet seemed sheepishly flattered and was, of course, at a complete loss for words.

"Well," I said," I don't understand it so I guess I'll just sit over here and be quiet. Sorry."

Janet continued, "The wise man built his house upon the rock...." Ben's face changed instantly from anger to glee as his little hands followed along and his eyes watched Janet's every move.

After Bible class, we all went to the auditorium for regular services and I told Gordon what had happened. "Well, I wonder what will happen when the entire congregation begins singing for song service this morning?" Gordon speculated.

Normally during church services, Ben would sit in the pew fairly well-behaved as long as he had something to keep him occupied such as puzzles or his Magna-Doodle® and never seemed to take much notice of the "grown-up" congregational singing. This day proved to be no different. Gordon, Dylan, Sarah, and I all participated in the song service as usual and Ben sat quietly engrossed in lining up his puzzle letters in neat little rows on the pew. He never even looked up when we all began singing. Gordon and I were thankful we had been spared another fit of rage but were nonetheless totally mystified.

****

The advent of autumn in Eastern Kentucky Appalachia came with its usual breathtaking display of color.

Dylan and Sarah were anxiously counting the days until Halloween and racking their brains trying to decide what costume to wear. Some friends from church had planned a Halloween party at their home for all the children, and Gordon and I decided we would give it a try since Benjamin probably wouldn't enjoy trick-or-treating, and candy was not appealing to him (unlike Dylan and Sarah).

Gordon had to work that evening, so I set out with my jail-bird, gypsy, and small black Halloween cat in tow. Our friends had decorated their garage for the games and festivities and all the children ran about talking and playing while the adults were coming in and out the adjoining door carrying plates loaded with hot dogs, chips, and cupcakes.

Benjamin had just awakened from his afternoon nap before we left and seemed quite bewildered by all the activity and the familiar voices that were unrecognizable to him decked out in Halloween garb.

After about thirty minutes, Ben wriggled out of my arms, walked past the group of ten or so toddlers without so much as a glance, and headed straight for the three concrete steps that led inside the house. I followed along behind him assuming he was just overtaken with curiosity about where exactly all these adults were coming and going from. Up the steps he went with my hands outstretched behind him for fear he would lose his balance and fall backward onto the concrete floor. Once safely inside the utility room, Ben immediately turned around and proceeded to go right back down the three steps.

Up. Down. Up. Down. Up. Down....

This quickly became quite annoying since adults were streaming in and out, and Ben and I were blocking the doorway. Ben was still too unsteady on his tiny feet to negotiate the big concrete steps without an adult's hand to hold on to. All attempts to redirect him were fruitless. I would carry Ben across the garage and set him down in the midst of the other happily munching toddlers and he would immediately jump up and go straight back to the steps. Exhausted, I finally sat down on the corner of the step as far out of everyone's way as possible and just let him continue with his fixation.

Dylan and Sarah were enjoying the party and were having a blast bobbing for apples with their friends, while Ben was having a blast with the steps.

All I could make of this behavior was that Ben was not accustomed to steps since we did not have any steps in the home we lived in at the time and was simply enjoying the novelty of it all.

Perseveration is an abnormal, obsessive interest in a single idea, activity, or person.

Two hours later, as the party was beginning to wind down, Ben the Halloween cat was still climbing up and down the steps with the same focus and fascination he had two hours before.

When it was time to leave, I had to physically carry Ben out to the car with him kicking and arching his back all the way. I fought to get him into his car seat without causing either of us bodily harm.

By this time, everyone from church was becoming accustomed to this type of outlandish behavior from Ben, and they graciously tried to act as if they didn't notice. I no longer felt as embarrassed in the presence of our church family, and was now simply resigned to just do the best I could at being a decent parent to this seemingly impossible child.

None of our close church friends were ever critical of Benjamin's behavior, at least not in our presence. I felt like they all knew from the way Dylan and Sarah had been reared in a structured and disciplined environment that it was likely that we simply had the misfortune of having an extremely difficult child.

Benjamin was a beautiful child, which in itself drew attention to the fact that he now was so disconnected from all those who had previously enjoyed holding, cuddling, and talking to him. Those church members who had always sat in the pews directly behind us were quick to notice that they could no longer engage Ben in silent games of peek-a-boo or other antics often quietly enjoyed with cute little babies during a sermon.

I was never completely sure if others felt sympathy, pity, or just tolerance for us and our "wild child." I decided that it really didn't matter how difficult it was becoming to survive a worship service because we were determined not to allow a severe case of bad behavior to keep us from the important business of serving God.

****

One Saturday afternoon in late October, brother Tol's wife, Dana, offered to baby-sit Benjamin for the afternoon so that Gordon and I could enjoy a quiet evening out. The opportunity for us to do so rarely presented itself anymore.

Dylan and Sarah were gone to their Dad's for the weekend, and Gordon had an unused vacation day. Knowing that Dana had always been Benjamin's favorite person, we decided it would be good for all our sakes to take her up on the offer and get out for a few hours by ourselves.

Dana had always taken the hard-line approach with all of our children and was swift to spoil but quick to discipline as well. All three of our children adored her.

We dropped Ben off at Tol and Dana's house with specific instructions on how to deal with the latest quirks, and as we were preparing to leave, I stood scanning my mind for every possible scenario that could possibly happen. Dana quickly interrupted me, "Oh good grief! Don't worry, he'll be fine! We'll find something fun to do and we'll deal with whatever happens. Now go on! Shoo! Have fun."

As we turned to leave, we noticed Ben just standing in the hallway staring at the pendulum on the grandfather clock.

"Bye, Ben!" I called from the porch.

He never took his eyes off the clock.

As we were pulling out of the driveway, I told Gordon, "You know, it's kind of good that Ben doesn't have a screaming fit when one of us leaves, but at the same time you'd kind of like to think that he misses us or realizes we're gone. Most kids his age cry after their parents, but Ben never does. Actually, now that I think of it, I haven't heard him even attempt to say 'Mama' or 'Dada' lately, have you?"

"No, honey, I haven't either. He'll be fine with Dana this afternoon. Let's just try to get out and enjoy ourselves for a few hours."

"Yeah. You're right, it seems like that's all we talk about anymore."

We drove an hour north to Richmond, the nearest mid-sized town with a reasonable selection of restaurants. After dinner, we decided to go to the mall and browse. On the way, we called to see how Dana was faring, just to be sure.

"Oh, he's fine. He just got up from his nap and we're outside. He seems to like running back and forth across the little sidewalk that connects the driveway to the front porch though. I'm not sure what's up with that, but as long as he's having fun, we're cool. No problem! Have fun!"

When we returned that evening, Dana informed us that Benjamin had continued to run back and forth across the sidewalk until she took him around to the back yard where he proceeded to run up and down a small hill of mulch that Tol was planning to use in his flower beds.

Many individuals with autism show limited understanding of social cues such as eye contact, facial expression, body language, or tone of voice.

"Not exactly the most conventional kind of play, but, oh well, he enjoyed it! But for some reason, I just can't get him to look at me and interact like he used to love to do. Must just be some kind of phase he's going through or something."

I noticed when we came in that Benjamin was sitting on top of their dog, Nina, thoroughly enjoying pulling her ears, which she didn't seem to mind, and he seemed as though he didn't notice that we had returned to pick him up.

When we got out to the van, Ben sat listlessly in his car seat looking out the window toward the night sky as if in deep thought. A lump formed in my throat as I fought back the tears. It wasn't my imagination. Dana had confirmed it as well.

Hearing another person mention the changes that were occurring in my child deepened my belief that the doctor just didn't understand when he brushed off my concerns. Something was wrong.

My beautiful baby seemed so far removed from me. Just capturing his fleeting glance with those intensely exquisite blue eyes was such a rare occasion that when it actually happened, it sent chill bumps down my spine. It was almost as if his eyes pierced through to my very soul.

I had mentioned to Gordon a few weeks earlier that I wasn't sure if Ben's intense, silent gaze made me feel so odd because it was so infrequent or if it was because it was just so deep and direct. Gordon said that he too had that feeling when Ben would suddenly lock eyes with him. He would look deep into his eyes for what seemed like forever. Never smiling, blinking, or reacting in any way. And then, just as suddenly, turn away and carry on with whatever he had been doing before.

Ben rode the few blocks to our home looking wistfully out the window the entire way.

"Wouldn't you just for once like to know what he's thinking about?" Gordon said quietly as he observed Ben in the rear-view mirror.

"Oh yes..." I sighed, "I'd give anything to know...."

He reminded me of a hurricane or a tornado...intensely beautiful, mysterious and powerful, yet unpredictable...and frighteningly out of control....

5

"And the prayer of faith will save the sick, and the
Lord will raise him up...." James 5:15 NKJV

On the first Thursday of November, Gordon called me at work to let me know that something was wrong with Ben.

"He got up from his nap with these little tiny bumps on his chest...almost looks like a heat rash or something."

"Does he have a fever or anything? Does he act like he feels bad at all?"

"No, no fever and he seems like he feels fine."

When I got home that afternoon, I pulled Ben's shirt up to examine the rash and noticed he now had the rash all over his back and some on his neck. He also was beginning to feel a little feverish.

Gordon said, "Wow, I just checked under his shirt less than an hour ago, and it looks much worse now. As a matter of fact, the little bumps look different now too...they did look like tiny little pimples earlier, now they are more like red bulls-eyes with white centers. How strange!"

Ben's temperature was 100.5. It was after 5 p.m. and I also knew Dr. Charles was out of town on a hunting trip. We decided to take Ben to the emergency room just in case this was an allergic reaction that needed medical attention.

I thought I had seen almost every kind of childhood illness, between my own children and those who had come into our office with various types of childhood infections, but this rash looked like nothing I had ever seen before. In many ways it resembled either erythema multiforme or Stevens-Johnson's Syndrome, both of which were extremely violent immune responses I had learned about in school. But the angry bull's-eye lesions were constantly migrating instead of remaining in the same location, which disqualified the rash from being either of these conditions.

By the time we arrived at the hospital, Benjamin's entire body was covered, including his scalp, face, and neck. It wasn't until I walked through the emergency room doors with Benjamin in my arms and saw the sheer look of panic on the faces of all those in the waiting area that I realized that we were only six weeks past the terror of September 11, 2001. Everyone had been living in fear of smallpox, anthrax, and any other unknown plague imaginable. Everyone stared fearfully at Ben, when it finally hit me what everyone was thinking.

I tried to explain, "We think it's just an allergy, but we'll just stand out in the hallway just in case, okay?"

A few of the wide-eyed patients slowly nodded their heads in agreement as Ben and I turned to go out to the hallway.

At that moment, Gordon was just returning from parking the car when the nurse whisked us back to an isolation room. I was thankful to have a private place to sit and let Ben lie down on the exam table since he was becoming increasingly irritable and tired.

The ER doctor arrived in an unusually prompt fashion decked out in protective gown, mask, and gloves and carefully examined Ben from head to toe. The doctor began asking questions such as if we had recently traveled, if Ben had ingested any new types of food, or if we had switched soaps or laundry detergents.

All of these questions were negative and the doctor, removing his gloves and mask, finally said, "Well I honestly don't know what it is, but I can say I don't think it's infectious. It's probably some kind of terrible allergic response to something."

As I listened, I suddenly remembered that Ben had a bad respiratory and ear infection about 2 ½ weeks before Halloween which had required a visit to Dr. Charles and a 10-day round of amoxicillin. It was now almost two weeks since he had finished his antibiotic, but I decided it was worth mentioning now to the ER doctor.

"Hmm," the doctor considered this, "it's not typical to have such a delayed response, but I guess it could possibly happen. Penicillin drugs are notorious for violent allergic responses. Was this the first or second time he has ever taken penicillin?"

Gordon and I thought back and counted that Ben had been sick enough to go to the doctor only a few times, and this was probably the third time he had taken amoxicillin - which wasn't that bad of a track record for an eighteen-month-old.

"We would have normally expected a response of this magnitude closer to the time he was actually taking the medication instead of two weeks afterward, but we can't rule it out just yet. Let's go ahead and run a battery of tests to positively rule out Lyme disease, Rocky Mountain spotted fever, and all those sorts of things just to be sure and we'll go from there."

The doctor left the room still in deep thought, and the lab technician arrived to do his dreaded duty. It took all three of us holding Ben to draw enough blood for that many tests. The more Ben cried, the more pronounced the angry bull's-eyes became. The lab tech finally left, and Ben lay in my arms whimpering. What on earth could it possibly be?

We waited for nearly four hours.

Every hour or so, the ER doctor would return with a colleague in tow and they would examine Ben again and discuss other possibilities. Each time, the rash had changed in appearance.

While the cause to date is unknown, a disproportionate number of children with autism have sensitivities or allergies to drugs, foods, and other environmental allergens.

Finally, at 1 a.m. the doctor returned to tell us that all the tests had come back negative and that he was still none-the-wiser on what it could be. He decided to give us two different oral medications, one a powerful antihistamine and the other an anti-itch medication.

The doctor reasoned that it had to be an immune response and that since Ben's lungs sounded reasonably clear, we could take him home for the night but return immediately if he developed any signs of respiratory distress, such as wheezing or swelling around the neck.

The next morning, Gordon arose early to go to work. Both of us had been up and down several times during the night to check on Ben, and he seemed to be sleeping peacefully.

As Gordon was leaving for work, he came into the bedroom to reassure me that he had just checked on Ben, that he was still sleeping, and looked about the same.

Thankful, I rolled back over and slept soundly for about two hours before I awoke to hear a small whimper coming across the baby monitor. I jumped out of bed and ran to Ben's crib to find him standing up, arms outstretched to be picked up, and looking completely unrecognizable!

The corners of his little mouth were down turned as he looked up at me through eyelids that were nearly completely swollen shut! I quickly lifted him from his crib and ran to the living room to get a better look at him in the morning light.

When I knelt down on the floor and tried to stand him up, Ben wobbled back and forth as if he couldn't stand. Looking down, I saw his tiny feet were swelled to twice their normal size! His neck was also badly swollen!

The angry red bull's-eyes were now three times the size they had been a few hours earlier, with each one now about the size of my hand. They were completely coalesced in such a way that he appeared to have been the victim of third degree burns over his entire body!

Panic stricken, I raced for the telephone and decided to call our good friend from church, Ray, who was also a family physician. As a general rule, we chose to use Ray only as a last resort since he would never take payment from us for his services, and we didn't want to burden him as our full-time physician.

Ray immediately admitted Benjamin to the hospital and ordered an IV line be set up in order to deliver steroids and Benadryl to ensure Ben's swollen neck did not block his airway.

It wasn't until I arrived at the hospital that I realized I was still in my pajamas and wearing only socks on my feet. At this point, I really didn't care. I asked one of the nurses to call Gordon and have him come straight to the hospital.

Gordon arrived in fifteen minutes, just in time for a team of five nurses to arrive to take Ben into an operating room so they could strap him down in order to get the IV line in. Two nurses had already come to the room to attempt to start the IV and were unable to do so due to Ben's wild thrashing, as well as the extent of the swelling in all of his extremities made it impossible to find a vein.

As the nurses carried Benjamin away, one of them turned back and said, "Don't worry, this will make it faster and easier for him and y'all if we do it this way."

As we listened to our terrified baby screaming down the hallway, the nurse's words seemed like small consolation, but we knew it was probably true.

We waited silently in an attempt to hear Benjamin crying from behind the closed doors at the other end of the floor. Over the usual hospital sounds of squeaking nurses' shoes and beeping monitors, we could ever so faintly hear Ben's frightened screams.

It felt like an eternity, but a few minutes later two of the nurses returned carrying a pathetic looking, whimpering Benjamin with a securely bandaged left foot.

"This was the only place we could find a vein, and we figured it would be the least likely place for him to try and pull it out..." offered one of the sweating and severely bedraggled nurses.

Debbie, the older head nurse, smiled and patted Ben on the back as I held his trembling little body in my arms and said in a thick northern accent, "Bless his little heart! He's been through a lot today! I don't blame it for being a wildcat."

Two other nurses soon returned pushing what looked like a huge metal cage with a mattress in it and parked it beside the regular hospital bed. Ben refused to lie down in either bed.

"You guys feel free to stay here around the clock if you like."

I appreciated the offer, but I wasn't about to leave my baby lying here in a metal cage all alone anyway, even if it had been against the rules!

Ray arrived within the hour and was quite shocked at Ben's appearance. He had reviewed all the notes and tests that had been run the day before in the ER.

Hospital stays are even more traumatic for children with autism due to change in routine, unfamiliar people, and the foreign and highly over-stimulating atmosphere.

"I think it is probably some kind of immune response as well, but we should run a few more tests just to exhaust every possibility. Does he look any better than he did before his first steroid injection?"

Looking at him, I said, "Actually...no. He looks about the same except for the pattern of the rash is constantly moving. It's like every time you look at him it's changed...."

Ray seemed just as puzzled as we were, yet we were thankful to have him overseeing Ben's hospital stay, knowing that Ray was a good Christian man whom we had known for years and that he would do everything he could to find out what was going on.

"We've started him out on a fairly high dose of steroids due to the swelling around his neck. His breathing seems to be stable, so we will gradually spread out the dose to wean him down and hope the IV Benadryl will help make him more comfortable. We'll get these tests and keep him here for a few days for observation until we're sure we're out of the woods."

We thanked Ray as he left and set about trying to get Ben comfortable. We lowered the side rail to the crib and pulled it up level with the hospital bed, but Ben refused to lie down in it. He refused to lie down on the regular bed as well.

First he wanted me to hold him, then Daddy, then back to me. Then he wanted down on the floor and became hysterical because we couldn't allow him to walk, or run for that matter, for fear of dislodging the IV in the top of his foot.

If I put him down on the bed, he would roll from side to side wildly flailing his arms and legs as he rolled. It was almost as if he were trying to get away from himself. He was totally inconsolable.

Gordon and I decided to try walking him up and down the hallways of our unit, each of us taking turns carrying him. This worked fairly well. It finally occurred to me to send Gordon down to the van to get our umbrella stroller so we could push him around instead of having to carry him since he seemed to be calmed in this way.

It seemed that every person we passed in the hallway had to stop and ask questions.

"What in the world happened to the poor baby?!"

"Oh my goodness! Has he been burned?!"

He was quite a sight to behold.

****

After three miserable days, we were still none the wiser.

Tol and Dana had arrived back from their vacation in Texas and rushed to the hospital the second they heard the news. I was strolling down the hallway for the thousandth time in three days when I heard Dana gasp, "Oh! My poor baby!! Oh! Just look at him!" Tears welled up into her eyes as she grabbed Ben out of my arms.

Ben, finally exhausted from his continuous battles with lab techs and nurses, nestled peacefully on Dana's shoulder. Tol and Dana took turns sitting with us for the rest of our stay and proved to be much comfort to me especially.

On the fourth day, Ray came around and explained the plan. "Well, all the tests have come back negative. I have spoken with an immunologist at the University of Kentucky and they too think it's an immune response, but we still don't know to what. The fact that the reaction has first improved then gotten worse, and improved again and gotten worse again, over the course of his hospital stay just doesn't make sense. If this were, in fact, a delayed response to the penicillin, one would logically expect the reaction to linearly improve over the course of his treatment with steroids and Benadryl since he is no longer being exposed to the penicillin. Instead it has fluctuated as if in response to something that he is being repeatedly exposed to even while here at the hospital. But you haven't given him any new foods, so we still are in the dark. His airway is okay, so we may send him home this evening if you can take him to the immunologist in the morning for a follow-up check."

Gordon took the suitcases down to the van, and I stood waiting outside our hospital room with Ben on my hip when Debbie, the head nurse, stopped to speak to Ben.

"Bye Sweetie..." she began.

Growling like an animal, Ben whipped around suddenly in my arms at the sound of her voice and violently threw himself backwards in a fit of rage. Taken off guard, I luckily was able to catch him before he fell to the floor.

The smile on Debbie's face was replaced by a look of dismay. Jumping to his defense, I said, "I guess he's still not quite feeling like himself."

Debbie smiled a fake smile, "I think we're just a little spoiled and could use a good pop on the hind end."

I felt my face flush hot with rage. How dare she say such a thing after all he'd been through!!

Just as I was opening my mouth to give her a piece of my mind, Gordon called out cheerily from down the hall, "We're all signed out! Come on, let's go home!"

I turned to walk away without saying a word and Debbie said smugly, "Good luck with that one."

"Therefore humble yourselves under the mighty hand of God, that He may exalt you in due time, casting all your care upon Him, for He cares for you."   1 Peter 5:6-7   NKJV

6

From the day we left the hospital, Benjamin was never the same. True, his behavior was gradually deteriorating before, but the changes that took place after were much more abrupt and noticeable. I wondered if perhaps the sheer trauma of the hospital stay had somehow scarred him emotionally....

It took over a month for the angry red bull's-eyes to completely fade.

The immunologist told us that after all the steroids and antihistamines, it was impossible to test for allergies. Even if he had not taken all the medications, the doctor felt the tests would likely have a poor outcome due to his young age and immature immune system. He advised keeping an emergency EpiPen® Jr. on hand at all times and giving him prescription antihistamines at the first sign of any allergic response in the future. We were to return for a full battery of allergy testing in about a year.

That entire winter was a misery. Benjamin's temper had become even more volatile, and he tantrumed at least two to three times per hour. If he wasn't tantruming, he was running back and forth looking over his shoulder as he ran or sitting completely withdrawn lining up his precious letters and numbers across the floor.

Deeply disturbed, the words of the nurse kept resonating in my mind, "just a little spoiled...." Gordon and I were good parents. I knew this for a fact. We had always taken great pains to work together as a consistent, unified parenting team. Dylan and Sarah both knew that whatever one of us said, the other backed 100%, and they knew it was a waste of time to argue otherwise.

When I was pregnant with Benjamin, Gordon and I had lengthy discussions about how there was to be no preferential treatment on either of our parts toward the new baby, no matter how long we had looked forward to his birth. After all, he was going to be the baby of the family by a whole nine years, and it would be very easy to make a brat out of him.

We also wanted to ensure that there would be no negative feelings toward the new baby on the part of the older children. Since Ben was Gordon's only child, we took great effort to ensure that all children in our home felt equally loved and valued, as well as equally disciplined. But sometimes even the best laid plans go awry....

At twenty months, I felt Ben was certainly old enough to understand the concept of "No!" But Ben didn't seem to even remotely understand any form of discipline, nor did he appear to understand anything that was said to him.

Most children are especially responsive to a stern look or tone of voice. Ben hardly seemed to notice.

Fear, be it rational fear or irrational, was entirely missing as well. Ben would often climb onto the arm of the couch or loveseat and leap off onto the floor without so much as a hesitation. His usual repertoire of running down the hallway looking over his shoulder was sometimes replaced with running as fast as he could down the hallway and shutting his eyes and continuing to run until he slammed into something. A fall or injury that would send most children crying to their mother for comfort didn't seem to faze Ben. If he was crying out in pain, it was because he was hurt very badly, if not bleeding.

Words were heard less and less these days. Most days they were entirely absent. Occasionally a new word would be uttered, only never to be heard again.

Each day at the office, all four of us would gather around the break room table to eat lunch and talk about the usual day to day events. That winter and spring, I was beginning to dread these conversations as Jennifer would chatter on and on about all the adorable things (two and three word phrases) Lauren had been saying.

During those early months of 2002, Jennifer and Michelle were beginning to make plans for the babies' upcoming birthday parties. One day over lunch, Jennifer asked, "So what kind of party are you guys gonna have for Ben this year?"

"I just don't know yet. We haven't even decided if we're going to have a big party again this year.... Ben just doesn't seem to like crowds as much as

Receptive language is the ability to understand communication. Expressive language is the ability to communicate using words, symbols, or gestures. Communication disorders are a classic hallmark of autism.

he used to." This ever-growing, sickening feeling was beginning to seem as if it would eventually engulf me. I felt maybe if I just didn't say it out loud it wouldn't be so. Whatever "it" was....

Even Michelle's little boy, Trevor, who was a full eleven months younger than Ben and Lauren was beginning to say a few words as well as respond receptively to verbal commands such as, "Get ball."

We were quickly becoming prisoners in our own home. Even a trip to the grocery store was a nightmare. More and more often, Gordon was carrying a screaming, thrashing Benjamin out during church services so that Tol could preach without having to compete with Ben's outbursts. Going out to eat was now completely out of the question, unless we felt like having all eyes riveted toward our table, giving judgmental glances and shaking their heads.

When Dr. Charles had seen Ben in the middle of October before his hospitalization, we had once again expressed concern over Ben's obvious lag in language as well as gesturing, but were again dismissed as overly worried parents. Dr. Charles insisted on waiting until closer to Ben's second birthday before becoming concerned.

Finally, at twenty-two months, I felt I could wait no longer. I asked Gordon to take Ben to see Dr. Charles for a routine checkup and told him to demand a referral...somewhere...anywhere...to check his hearing or *something*. I sent Gordon by himself thinking that Dr. Charles was beginning to think I had become a neurotic mother. However I had to go about it, I was determined to get some kind of answers.

Gordon prevailed and Dr. Charles' nurse set up an evaluation to take place in three weeks by an Ear, Nose, and Throat Specialist in Richmond, some fifty miles north of us. I felt quite certain there was nothing wrong with Ben's hearing, other than it seemed to be selective. But I still felt relief that this was at least a start.

****

The day finally arrived and Gordon, Benjamin, and I headed north to see Dr. Anders. As an afterthought, Gordon and I had decided to take an extra day off and go on up to Cincinnati to take Ben to the zoo the day before his appointment.

On the way to the zoo, we stopped at a shopping mall to pick up some items for the children and happened upon a large play area inside the mall. The playground was designed in a prehistoric style, with a four-foot high "stone" archway at the entrance. At least 150 toddlers and preschoolers were running, climbing, and jumping about the playground. Gordon and I decided to let Ben play for awhile to burn off some energy after the long car ride.

Ben looked at the archway as if totally amazed. Suddenly, he bolted through the archway with his characteristic sideways look over his shoulder. Smiling and laughing, Ben continued to run through the archway and seemed to be fascinated with the fact that he could not only track the archway with his eyes from the side, but also from above. Pleased that Ben was enjoying himself, we stayed for two hours. We never made it to the zoo. A worn out but happy Benjamin finally crawled into his stroller and fell fast asleep.

How could it be that Ben never once noticed a single other child in the play area? He had run through the archway for two hours, constantly bumping into other children, often even knocking them off their feet and had never acknowledged a single one of them.

While complicated for any parent, dealing with medical professionals is even more complicated for parents of children with autism. It is crucial to find health care providers who understand the needs of children on the autism spectrum.

****

The next day, we arrived at the doctor's office, and I nervously filled out a chart. One question read "Reason for your visit."

I wrote, "Hearing check."

How ridiculous was it to be testing a child's hearing that could hear the theme song to Elmo's World from a half a block away? What was I thinking?

The nurse took us back and proceeded to ask more questions, "How many words does Benjamin say?"

"You mean how many has he ever said or how many does he say now?" The nurse gave me an odd look, "How many does he regularly use...forty?... fifty? Just give me a ballpark figure."

Gordon and I looked at each other, "I don't know.... Maybe... four?... five?"

"You said he was how old?" rifling through her papers, "twenty-three months? That's not right. What words *does* he say?"

"Well, he sometimes says other words, but you usually never hear them again, but lately he's been saying the numbers 'five,' 'six,' 'four,' 'nine' and the word 'stop'...but that's only when he sees this certain game show where they slam the buzzer and yell, "Stop!""

Now that I had heard myself say all this aloud, I began to realize the severity of it all. Hearing a healthcare worker say the words, "That's not right," in reference to my child's development made my palms sweat and my mouth feel dry.

I stammered, "We've been worried about him for some time.... But everyone keeps telling us he'll talk when he's ready.... We've really been working with him...but he just doesn't seem interested...."

I realized that I didn't want this woman to think we were negligent parents who were oblivious to their child's obvious deficits.... We weren't stupid.... No one would listen to us.... The nurse smiled sympathetically and said, "Dr. Anders will be here in a few minutes and talk with you."

Dr. Anders was a tall, bespectacled, silver-haired man with an air of solemnity. "Hello, Mr. and Mrs. Liske," he said as he entered without ever looking up from the chart. "So I understand you are here with concerns about your child's hearing?"

Dr. Anders sat down on his rolling doctor's stool and thumbed through Ben's chart.

"Well, yes. I suppose," I answered, "it's more because he just doesn't seem to be talking as much as he should." I felt as if I were talking to myself, since Dr. Anders still refused to make eye contact with either Gordon or myself.

Dr. Anders arose from his seat, "Um-hmm. It says here that this child is twenty-three months old and says five words, is that correct?" Benjamin had been seated in his stroller beside me busily drawing on his travel-size Magna-Doodle®, equally as removed from our conversation as Dr. Anders seemed.

"Yes, that's right."

Dr. Anders then took what appeared to be a small ball of crumpled cellophane from the pocket of his white lab coat and ever so softly crinkled it between his thumb and forefinger as he held it approximately two feet from the back of Benjamin's head. First off to the left and then off to the right.

Benjamin briefly glanced up from his Magna-Doodle® each time Dr. Anders crinkled the cellophane. Ben turned his head each time in the direction from which the sound had been produced.

Next, Dr. Anders examined Ben's ears. Ben resisted, kicking and screaming wildly in Gordon's arms. "His ears look good," Dr. Anders stated after returning to his stool and beginning to write some notes in Ben's chart, "and there is nothing to lead me to believe that your child has any hearing problems. We will have him come back in a few weeks to do a formal hearing screening in a sound chamber just to positively rule out any problems. Children who are totally deaf even attempt to communicate in some way by gesturing or pointing. You need to consider some form of autism."

With that, Dr. Anders was finished with his examination and rose from his stool putting his ink pen in his breast pocket as if there were nothing left to say or do.

What did he just say?

"Excuse me...wait..." stunned, I heard myself say in desperation, "What are you talking about? Where do we go? Who do we see?"

Almost annoyed, Dr. Anders said, "We don't deal with that here. The receptionist at the desk might be able to pull up a phone number for the early intervention program. I think it might be called 'First Steps.' Check with her."

With that, he left. Just like that. When the door swung shut behind him, I felt as if the door to Benjamin's entire future had just slammed shut as well.

These pictures were taken in the last few months before Ben's diagnosis. He's participating in two of his favorite self-stimulatory activities - lining up magnetic letters on the front of the stove and watching the water run at the kitchen sink.

"But He said to them, "Why are you fearful, O you of little faith?...." Matthew 8:26 NKJV

7

To this day, I still do not remember checking out at the front desk, leaving the building, or walking out to the van. "What is autism, anyway?" asked Gordon as we pulled out of the parking lot.

Shaken from my daze, I realized Gordon was entirely unaware of the magnitude of what had just transpired, "Don't you remember that movie 'Rain Man'? That's what he had. I don't know if that's the way people with autism act in real life, but I'd almost swear that Dr. Anders had autism himself, monotone voice, zero personality and all. Did you notice he never once looked us in the eye?"

I felt shortchanged for having paid for the quality of bedside manner we had received.

"Yeah, I noticed that too. Hmm..." Gordon said, "Might take one to know one."

I supposed at least now we had something tangible to work with, even though I was still too unclear about what autism really was to know how upset I should actually be. Not quite sure what to do, I had a nagging sense of urgency that I needed to take matters into my own hands. Pulling my cell phone from the diaper bag, I called Tol.

"Tol, it's me, Juli. Listen, we're just now leaving Ben's doctor's appointment up in Richmond, and this doctor seems to think Ben might have some kind of autism. Could you do me a favor and get online and pull up anything you can find about autism and what the symptoms are?"

We did not have a home computer at the time, and sensing the urgency in my voice Tol said, "Okay...I'll get right on it right now."

Next, I called Dr. Charles' office. "Gail, this is Juli. This ENT doctor you guys sent us to thinks Ben might have autism and says that we should talk to some kind of state program called First Steps. I don't have time to stand around and wait for the government to get around to evaluating my child in a month or so. We want answers now. Can you ask Dr. Charles where we can go to be seen now? We don't care if we have to pay out-of-pocket."

Dr. Charles was apparently standing nearby. Gail said, "Hang on a second." I could hear her relay the message. Silence.

"Dr. Charles says he will call the University of Kentucky's psychiatry department and find out where he can be seen just as soon as we hang up. I'll call you right back and tell you what we found out."

I was relieved that Dr. Charles was actually cooperating for once lately. I thanked her and as I was preparing to hang up, Gail said, "Gee, I hope little Ben doesn't have that...surely not...."

I hoped not either.

As we drove southward through the mountains, a dusty coal truck lumbering along in front of us, both Gordon and I were lost in thought. I was trying to think back through all the patients with different disabilities I had seen over the years. How common was autism anyway? Did I even know anyone who knew anyone who had it?

Autism occurs four to five times more often in boys than in girls.

I suddenly remembered one little boy about ten or eleven years old. His mother had brought him in for a checkup and as I recalled, I couldn't even get him to sit in the chair. He insisted upon flipping the light switch off and on...off and on...all the while jumping up and down with glee, flapping his hands, and jabbering some kind of unintelligible jargon... kind of like the jabbering I had heard Ben do from time to time....

Finally, after much unsuccessful coaxing, his mother and I decided it would be in everyone's best interest to refer him to a pediatric dentist to be treated under sedation. But that little boy had such a spaced-out look about him...almost a kind of insane look. Benjamin didn't look like that.

Or did he?

As I turned to look at Ben, I was startled by the ring of my cell phone. It was Dana's voice on the other end, "Tol just told me what that doctor said. He doesn't know what he's talking about! Benjamin *does not* have autism! Sure, he may be a little delayed in speech, but he doesn't need special-ed or anything. That's where they stick kids like that you know...."

"I certainly hope he doesn't know what he's talking about either," I said, "but could you have Tol call me after he finds some stuff online, okay?"

"Okay...but I still don't think he knows what he's talking about. Love you."

When we got home there was already a message on the answering machine from Gail asking me to call her back.

"UK's Department of Psychiatry says that there is a special evaluation center affiliated with UK that does these kinds of evaluations on children under the age of three. I called them and set up an evaluation for nine days from today on Tuesday, April 23rd at 9 a.m. That's the very first available appointment. Will that work?"

"Sure, we'll make it work. Nine days seems like an eternity, but I guess that *is* quick."

Gail said, "They told me the evaluation would take up to three hours, maybe longer. They had several questions about Benjamin's behavior and all that I didn't feel qualified to answer, so I told them I'd have you call them back."

I got the impression from Gail's tone of voice that she felt as if Dr. Charles had dropped the ball on this one, and I could tell she felt really bad about it.

"Thanks for all your help, Gail."

As I was about to hang up, Gail gushed, "I wish you all the best of luck. I just think so much of you and your family. Please let me know what they say."

When I called the evaluation center, a pleasant sounding young woman answered the phone. "Yes, Mrs. Liske, we just needed to ask a few questions in preparation for Benjamin's appointment and let you know what to expect when you come for his evaluation."

After answering the woman's questions about Ben's speech and language development as well as a host of other seemingly unrelated questions about Ben's sleeping, eating, and play habits, I anxiously asked, "Does it sound like he really might have autism?"

I must have sounded hopelessly desperate. I knew full well that the young woman was in no position to answer such a question; she *was* just the secretary. That would be like asking our secretary, Michelle, to diagnose an abscessed tooth over the telephone. I just wanted to know something...NOW.

"Well, Mrs. Liske, it does sound as if he needs an assessment. We have a great team here who will conduct a thorough multi-disciplinary evaluation covering all domains of development. He will be seen by a developmental-behavioral pediatrician, a general pediatrician, a speech and language pathologist, a physical therapist, and a psychologist. They each will conduct their assessments, one at a time, in the same special room that is designed to make your child feel comfortable and able to behave in a manner as close as possible to his usual behavior. The room is carpeted and has lots of toys to choose from. It also has a two-way viewing mirror from which the other examiners will observe while each examiner is conducting their assessment. You and Mr. Liske are more than welcome to stay in the room with him in order for him to feel more relaxed and at home. At the end of all the evaluations, the team will reconvene to discuss their findings and will render a diagnosis, if applicable, before you leave that day."

I decided to spend the next eight days busily gathering information in order to be equipped to ask questions at the evaluation, as well as to pass the time without losing my mind.

Early the next morning after I had already left for work, Tol brought Gordon a stack of information he had gathered from the internet.

A parent's persistent attitude can make all the difference in gaining months, or even years, of precious time through early diagnosis.

During lunch, I contacted First Steps to see what kind of services they offered as well as to see if anything could be accomplished while we were waiting for the evaluation. The woman I spoke with sounded surprised that we had an appointment for an evaluation, stating that the normal chain of events was for the child's pediatrician or family physician to contact First Steps when a disability was initially suspected.

First Steps was then to come out to the home and conduct a point of entry referral, she explained, and arrange for the child to be evaluated by First Steps therapists if the point of entry person felt it warranted based on the first impressions gathered at that initial home visit. These evaluations were to be conducted within thirty days of the original referral.

The information gathered during these evaluations was to determine if the child was, in fact, at significant risk and needed a higher level evaluation, at which point First Steps would arrange for the child to be seen at either of two testing centers located in Lexington or Louisville.

"That's odd," the woman said, "How did you manage to get an appointment with UK without going through us first?"

I really didn't see why it mattered. Perhaps the lady felt as if I had somehow "cut line" in the process of bureaucratic red tape.

The lady said, "I guess based on what your doctor told UK over the phone, they must have deemed the problem severe enough to go ahead without a due process referral." Somehow I didn't translate my untimely speed in obtaining an appointment with UK as necessarily a good thing. It sounded more ominous than I cared to face at this point.

"Since UK has already agreed to see your child, I suppose that automatically qualifies him as being 'at risk,' therefore qualifying him for First

Steps services. All I need to do is call UK and verify your appointment. We'll send somebody out Friday to bring you the necessary paperwork to get the ball rolling."

I supposed I should have felt privileged that my child was so obviously damaged that he was able to circumvent the usual lengthy process of accessing government services. I was beginning to feel numb.

What had actually happened was my child's physician thought I was a hypochondriac with nothing better to do than invent imaginary problems for my child, and he was now being forced to eat crow and pull every string available in order to try and rectify the situation. In plain English, *that* is exactly what happened.

However, I kept these thoughts to myself and supposed I should simply be thankful that things were falling into place as quickly as they were. It didn't matter how things were being expedited, just that they were...finally.

As a fellow human being, I still liked Dr. Charles. He had bent over backwards these last few days to help make up for lost time. This just happened to be yet another case in point of the medical profession's failure to carefully consider each patient as an individual and to recognize that, from time to time, parents actually do know something. Parents may not know what that "something" is; often they just know something is not right with their child. They at least deserve to be heard and taken seriously.

When I got home that evening, I grabbed up the information Tol had collected and devoured every page. The more I read, the more hopeless I began to feel.

The first page was a simple autism checklist called the CHAT (Childhood Autism Test) that is to be administered by a child's physician at his routine eighteen-month checkup. It couldn't be much simpler. The test was designed in such a way that any physician could easily use it. With nine simple yes/no questions and no more than two to three minutes, a practitioner could recognize the early warning signs of autism and related disorders, thereby preventing the loss of months, sometimes years, of valuable early intervention time.

Questions like: "Does your child take an interest in other children?"

"Does your child use his index finger to point, to ask for something?"

"Does your child ever bring objects over to show you something?"

As I read over the checklist, I realized that in the case of Benjamin, the answer to every question was not the answer it should have been.

I felt too numb to cry. Could this really be happening? When was I going to awaken from this nightmare and find the happily gurgling, lovable baby pictured in the early pages of Ben's baby book? Where did he go? When exactly did he leave? Why had this dreaded soul-snatcher called autism come and taken my beautiful, blue-eyed baby?

Just then, the telephone rang. It was Dana. "Did you happen to get a chance to look at those papers Tol brought over to Gordon this morning?"

"Actually, I just got home and sat down to look at them. Did you read them?"

"...Yeah, I did." Somehow Dana didn't sound nearly as optimistic as she had the day before. "After reading through all the material...now I'm not so sure anymore. Benjamin does do a lot of the things that were mentioned in those pages. But, Juli, you know," Dana was now trying to sound more upbeat, "all of us have *some* of those traits. For crying out loud! I know I have a bunch of them and so does Tol. I don't know of anybody more obsessive/compulsive than me. Actually, the more I read, I was beginning to think maybe Tol was autistic! I suppose the determining factor is not whether anybody has *some* of the traits, but rather if they have all or most of the traits...."

I genuinely appreciated Dana's attempts to humor me. Dana was a large, yet attractive woman, with a gorgeous smile and a contagious laugh. She always had a knack for encouragement, especially during a person's darkest hour.

"We're just gonna have to pray about it, Sweetie. Always remember, God *is* in control. I know it doesn't seem like it right now, but He is. If Benjamin really is autistic, then that's God's plan, and everything will work itself out. You've just gotta believe that. Okay? Your family really needs you now more than ever. You just do what you gotta do and let God take care of the rest. Don't make yourself sick over this. Got it? We'll call and check on you tomorrow."

"Why do you stand afar off, O Lord?
Why do You hide Yourself in times of trouble?"
Psalm 10:1 NKJV

8

Friday came and the person from First Steps, Ms. Miller, arrived to collect the pertinent information required before the therapists could make their home visits to determine Benjamin's current level of functioning.

Benjamin was napping when Ms. Miller arrived, "Do you need me to wake him?" I asked.

"Oh, no need," she said, "you can just tell me the things I need to know about Benjamin."

Once again, I got the distinct impression that all these people had already decided that Ben did, in fact, have autism, without even meeting him. After sitting through an hour of bureaucratic jargon about things such as IFSP's, IEP's, POE's, and PSC's, Ms. Miller informed me that as soon as Benjamin's UK evaluation was completed next week, she would be back out with a list of the different therapists for me to choose from.

"So based on the information I just gave you, you really think Ben has autism too, don't you?" I asked flatly. Taken off guard, Ms. Miller said, "It's really not my place to say...but after having done this job for over twenty years and based on what you've said...just between you and me...." she slowly nodded her head.

At this point, I appreciated her candor. It was time to stop trying to fool myself.

"I guess it's time for me to face the inevitable and get along with the business of finding out everything I can to help Ben." I felt strangely disconnected from myself and felt as if a "mother's emergency auto-pilot switch" had been activated causing my mouth to speak and keeping my emotions in check in order to deal with the crisis at hand.

Ms. Miller looked at me sympathetically "...and I can tell you're the kind of parent who will do just that. Most parents I've dealt with don't seem to have the same kind of tenacity and determination I can see in you. Ben is fortunate to have you and your husband as his parents."

For the first time in over a month, I felt a strange sense of peace, almost a kind of closure.

Now that I almost had a name for what was wrong with my child, I could prepare to take this proverbial bull by the horns, but first I had to learn about the nature of this bull I was planning to tackle.

Both Gordon and I were almost entirely computer illiterate at that time and relied heavily on Tol and Dana as well as many others to do our internet surfing while I scoured the bookstores and library. I had already read the material that Tol had brought over earlier and was convinced that there must be more knowledgeable, as well as more optimistic resources to be found.

As with any major life trauma, the feelings of denial, shock, helplessness, guilt, anger, grief, resentment, and acceptance are associated with a child or grandchild's diagnosis of autism.

This original information basically said that autism was definitely on the rise, there was no known cause, there was no cure, 75% are mentally retarded, 50-70% never speak, and the majority live out their adult lives and ultimately die in institutions.

I may not have known a whole lot about autism, but I did know one thing. If they, whoever "THEY" were, couldn't tell me what caused autism, then THEY weren't going to tell me there WASN'T anything I could do to fix it. I decided then that I wasn't going to accept anything THEY said and just take it lying down. THEY obviously didn't have a child with autism!

Wasn't this supposed to be the twenty-first century? With all the advances in medicine, how could the medical community be *completely* in the dark on a disorder that is so obviously on the rise? And on top of that, not particularly seem to care?

I could see it now...the government and all the national networks and newspapers would be all abuzz, working round the clock, if some kind of aliens had landed and begun snatching American toddlers by the thousands right out of their own homes, never to be seen again...like some kind of "Invasion of the Brain Snatchers."

I could just visualize it. The FBI would be working night and day! The president would have issued a full "Amber Alert." There would be roadblocks, swat teams....

Couldn't they see? This was a full-blown epidemic, and I hadn't even heard that autism was on the rise until this week!

What was the difference? These babies were literally being stolen by the thousands with their lives being rendered useless by a culprit that was rapidly becoming bolder and bolder, and no one, except maybe their parents, seemed to care!

I went to the public library and checked out the only two books they had on autistic spectrum disorders. The first book I read was equally depressing as the first material. This particular book even had a copyright date of the year 2000. Its main suggestions for treatment were state-funded early intervention services (which included only a few, if not just one hour of each prescribed therapy per week), drug therapy using major tranquilizers, or a combination of both of the above.

Towards the end of this book, it mentioned almost in passing, a controversial kind of therapy called ABA, or Applied Behavior Analysis, as being an approach that some had suggested as being highly effective but that was often considered to be an unattractive alternative due to its being a time-consuming and costly program (thirty-five to forty hours per week).

That did sound like a large amount of time to spend in therapy, but if it really helped your child, I was sure it would be worth it. The book did not further elaborate on how the program worked, what kind of results had been achieved before, or where to go to find out more.

****

When I wasn't buried in a book or trying to manage Ben, I was at work. Jennifer, Pam, and Michelle seemed as though they were afraid to say much to me about the upcoming evaluation, and when they did, it was always an attempt to be optimistic.

One morning as I was sitting next to Michelle at the reception desk awaiting the arrival of my first patient, Michelle offered, "I wish you'd stop lookin' so depressed."

Michelle, bless her heart, in her usual countrified way said, "I'm not real sure what it is, but I don't think Ben's artistic!"

Pam, overhearing, interjected "It's not ARtistic, Stupid! It's AUtistic!"

Completely accustomed to being grammatically chastised, Michelle said, "I'm sorry. Whatever it is, I don't think Ben has it. What makes 'em think he does?"

I tried my best to explain to Michelle what exactly autism was and that she hadn't been around Benjamin enough lately to see how he had changed.

"Well..." now beginning to doubt herself, "if he does, then hopefully it's just mild."

Both of our families simply did not want to accept the possibility that Benjamin might have autism. My father and Gordon's mother, particularly, seemed to be having a difficult time even understanding what autism was.

Both said, "Well...if he DOES have that, there's NEVER been anybody on OUR side of the family with anything like that." Both being from the old school, they had the misconception that autism was some sort of shameful mental illness that families kept secret. Neither Gordon nor I were willing to participate in these sorts of blame games.

If this is what he has, what difference did it make whose gene pool was responsible?!? With both of us being exhausted both mentally as well as physically, we decided it was probably best not discuss it any further with family until we knew something for sure.

Dylan and Sarah were beginning to realize something was going on with all the phone calls, late night discussions, and the general somber mood hanging like a black cloud.

One afternoon that week we were all out in the yard enjoying the first warm days of spring. Gordon and I were setting out spring flowers. Dylan and Sarah were tagging along watching and asking questions. Benjamin was running back and forth across the yard tracking first the dogwood tree, then Sarah with his eyes.

Sarah asked, "Why in the world does Ben do that?! He looks so weird! Hey. You know that little red-haired kid at church? Janet's little boy, Alex? I noticed he talks a whole lot more than Ben, and he says the cutest stuff! Why doesn't Ben? Didn't you guys take him to the doctor for that here lately or somethin'?"

Glancing over at Gordon, I hesitated, "Well, we still have to go see some more doctors next week to see what's up. We're not sure yet...." Realizing I was going to have to tell them something sooner or later and not wanting them to hear it from someone else, I asked, "Do you guys have anybody that you know of at your school who has autism?"

"Whatdaya mean," Dylan said, "autistic?"

I nodded, "Yes."

"Yeah, there's this one kid named Josh I see sometimes. Everybody knows him. He acts real wild and stuff and sings all the time just whenever and wherever and jumps up and down and screams a lot too. But he never talks for real, just sings. Why do you ask?"

It had already crossed my mind that it may be particularly traumatic for two adolescents to discover that their sibling has a disability, especially one so stigmatizing. Kids in this age bracket seem to be particularly sensitive to anything that might make them or their families appear to be "uncool." I decided that now might be a good time to start feeling them out.

"Well, we won't know for sure until next week. But yes, he might have something like that."

Sarah exclaimed, "Oh my gosh, Mom! I don't want Ben to have that! How embarrassing!"

Surprised, I looked at her and said, "What do you want us to do about it? Give him away?"

Sarah looked suddenly sheepish and ashamed of herself, "Well no! But does that mean he's gonna act like Josh?"

Trying to sound reassuring, Gordon said, "We don't know anything for sure yet, but all kids with autism don't necessarily act that way. We are all just going to have to work together and try to make the best of it. He's still your baby brother, and we know you'll love him just the same."

It is important to recognize and validate the feelings of siblings of a child with autism. Careful listening and observation are necessary in order to do this.

Both children nodded in agreement. Sarah, affectionately ruffling Ben's hair as he ran past, said, "Yeah, we love 'im; I guess we'll have to keep 'im."

9

"Save me, O God! For the waters have come up to my neck.
I sink in deep mire, Where there is no standing; I have come into
deep waters, Where the floods overflow me. I am weary with my
crying; My throat is dry; My eyes fail while I wait for my God."

Psalm 69:1-3   NKJV

April 23, 2002. After getting the older children off to school, Gordon and I loaded Benjamin into the van and headed north to Lexington. It was a beautiful spring day with the mountains splashed with the color of the blooming redbud trees. I had always loved this time of year with all the flowering trees, colorful tulips, newborn foals and calves in the fields, and the children's eager anticipation for the ending of another school year and the temporary freedom it brings.

This particular morning, however, was filled more with an ominous dread combined with a wish just to have the inevitable over and done with. Gordon and I traveled at least the first twenty miles in silence. Benjamin sat in his car seat quietly gazing out the side window and looking strikingly handsome with his navy pique polo shirt, khaki dress pants, and rosy cheeks. Although I had never been one to be particularly materialistic, I found myself in recent months taking great pains to ensure that Ben was always impeccably groomed and dressed to perfection. Perhaps subconsciously I felt he would be less likely to be rejected due to his often outlandish behavior if he looked more appealing. I suppose it's easier for strangers to tolerate a difficult child if he smells good and looks nice. Don't ask me how I developed the line of reasoning; it just seemed right at the time.

As we passed a large pasture full of cows, two bright white-washed looking new calves caught my eye as they jumped and frolicked among the dingy, slow-moving adult cows.

"Oh look how cute..." I remarked, "isn't it weird how happy and full of energy the brand new ones are, only to grow up and find out how depressing their lives really are?"

Gordon gave me an odd glance, "Sounds depressing to me. What made you say that, Baby?"

I sighed, "Oh, I don't know. I guess that's just the frame of mind I'm in today. Sorry."

Gordon could sense that it would probably be best for my mental health to try and get a conversation started at this point. "What do you think the doctors are going to tell us today? Really. Do you think they are going to say that Ben has autism?"

I realized that it would probably be best for both of us to air our feelings now and prepare one another for every possibility that had crossed our minds. "Really?" I said, forcing a smile, "really I hope they're just going to tell us our child is the worst brat they ever saw and that otherwise he's okay...but yeah...I think they're going to tell us he has autism."

Gordon reached over and clasped my hand tightly in his, "Me too, Baby... me too..." Hearing Gordon say that aloud, I yearned to lay over in his arms and let the floodgates open for the first time since this whole ordeal began nine days before.

Not sure if Ben would react to such an outburst, and not wanting to negatively influence his performance at the evaluation, I stared straight ahead at the horizon and choked back the tears with a painful lump in my throat and a knot in my stomach. I knew that if I looked at Gordon or Benjamin, it would all be over with. I would start to cry, and at this point I wasn't sure if once I started, I would ever be able to stop.

When we finally arrived at the evaluation center, Gordon parked the van, and we paused before getting out offering yet another prayer of petition to God. I knew that our God had not forsaken us. He had, in fact, blessed us with this beautiful child to love.

Gordon finished, "...and above all, Lord, help us always remember that it is not our will, but rather Your will that should be done...."

As we opened the doors to get out, I nervously rationalized out loud, "Well, at least we know that if it's God's will that he can never take care of himself...that his soul will always be perfect and that it belongs to God. His life here on earth may have been stolen from him, but his life after will always be perfect..." tears springing to my eyes. Gordon nodded in agreement as he solemnly unbuckled Ben's car seat.

That thought gave me the strength to get up and go on.

****

The evaluation center was a satellite building in a different part of town than the rest of the university. We entered into a tiny waiting room and sat all alone on the couch until the same pleasant sounding woman I had spoken to on the phone came to the door and greeted us.

"This must be Benjamin," she said cheerily. "Just fill out this registration form and we'll be ready to get started."

The evaluation room was exactly as I had imagined. The behaviorist, pediatrician, psychologist, and therapists all entered and greeted us warmly and gave a brief explanation of how the evaluation was to proceed.

Since autism is such a complex disorder, a multidisciplinary approach is best to ensure a comprehensive picture of the "whole child" in obtaining an accurate diagnosis.

Dr. Frost, the pediatrician, and the behaviorist, Dr. Benge, stayed in the room while the other examiners left to observe from behind the two-way mirror. Dr. Frost began by taking a very detailed history beginning with the pregnancy and continuing through every aspect of Benjamin's growth, development, behavior, etc. as well as a family and social history.

Dr. Benge seemed to sit along the sidelines and observe Ben's activities while Dr. Frost conducted our interview. Dr. Frost was quite a young man with dark hair and glasses. He seemed to have a very warm and caring manner and appeared to be taking much thought in his line of questioning.

Dr. Benge was very interested in watching Ben with his one and only most prized possession of all time...his Magna-Doodle®, which he stealthily lifted from the diaper bag that had been sitting on the floor at my feet. Dr. Benge was an older woman, about mid-fifties, with long silver-streaked hair that was swept up into a graceful bun. She had strikingly beautiful light blue eyes and carried herself in a gentle motherly manner. Every so often, she would unobtrusively attempt to introduce some other type of toy to Ben by setting them close into his field of view. Ben, without even looking up at her or the toy, would firmly take his Magna-Doodle® in hand and turn his back to her and proceed with his scribbling.

One by one, each therapist came in to do their segment of the evaluation. Gordon and I sat off to the side helplessly watching as if glued to a suspenseful movie. It felt as if I were trying to somehow telepathically prompt Ben to perform the actions we knew the therapists were fishing for.

The therapists each made a point to sit on the floor and attempt to build rapport with Ben, who was still adamant about maintaining his grip on his Magna-Doodle®. Finally, I reached over and took it from him, but not without fierce resistance, feeling that perhaps Ben might be more amenable to participating appropriately without it. I was wrong.

When the psychologist brought forth a doll and a handful of Cheerios and began to model pretending to feed the baby, Ben ignored her. He reached over and grabbed as many Cheerios as he could, and ate them himself.

When asked, "Where's Mommy?" or "Where's the ball?" Benjamin acted as though no one had spoken.

When the examiners said his name during the evaluation, he did not respond. Gordon and I knew that Benjamin was failing the test with flying colors.

The last examiner left the room to join the others in the conference room leaving the three of us alone. Uncertain how long it would take, we were surprised when Dr. Frost and Dr. Benge returned in less than fifteen minutes to talk with us. Both doctors gave us a sympathetic-looking smile as they entered, my heart began to pound as they each silently pulled up a chair to sit directly facing Gordon and me in an oddly close fashion with our knees practically touching when they sat down. I knew this could be nothing other than bad news, if not the very worst. I was sitting on the inside in the corner and felt quite cramped. It was as if they were attempting to corral me in.

Dr. Frost spoke first. Sighing, he gave me a kind look and said, "After tabulating all the data collected today, we have determined that Benjamin has autism."

There. It had been said. Gordon, having my hand clutched in his, seemed to wince and began to nervously rub my hand between his. I felt totally paralyzed. Even though I thought I was prepared and felt reasonably certain of what the diagnosis would be, nothing could have prepared me for the way I felt at that moment.

He hadn't said, "*might* have autism," or "we *think* it could be possible...."

There seemed to be no doubt, no glimmer of possibility. I looked over toward the other corner where Benjamin sat quietly scribbling on his Magna-Doodle®. All the hopes, dreams, and aspirations for our handsome son had been terminated just barely after they were supposed to be beginning.

Dr. Benge broke the silence, "How do you all feel about that?" she asked gently.

My ability to speak having momentarily disappeared, Gordon spoke quietly, "We kind of thought that's what you might say.... We've been doing some reading this past week but are still kind of at a loss for what to do next."

"Well, that's what we're here for, to answer any questions you might have," Dr. Benge said.

I couldn't see how she could bear to do this for a living.

Finding my voice, I said in a low, hoarse voice, "So how bad is it? Is it severe?"

Some statistics state that a full 75-80 percent of persons with autism score in the mentally retarded range (generally an IQ below 68-70 on most standardized tests). However, it is important for parents to keep in mind that standardized IQ tests do not take into consideration the unique learning differences of the ASD population.

Dr. Benge looked at Dr. Frost as if begging for a bail out.

Dr. Frost, fidgeting nervously with his stethoscope, "We don't normally like to 'rate' the children we see in that way. They are all so very different from one another it's hard to say...but Benjamin does show some potential...even though he doesn't say but a few words, he does use a lot of jargoning...that's a start...." His explanation seemed rather weak, at best.

Dr. Benge interrupted, "Robin, our clinic coordinator, is filling out a handwritten description of the services we are prescribing for Benjamin and you and your physician will each receive a formal, detailed report of this evaluation in a couple of weeks. In the meantime you can be getting started with First Steps to get his therapies started as soon as possible."

As if on cue, Robin appeared at that moment and handed Gordon the paper along with a packet. "The packet has a list of helpful resources available throughout the state as well as support group contacts," Robin explained.

Looking at the paper, I read under the category for diagnoses: "Autism, significant language delay, probable cognitive delay (scores were not obtainable)."

I searched Dr. Benge's face for an explanation, "What do you mean 'probable cognitive delay'? You think he might be...mentally retarded or something too?"

Dr. Benge quickly said, "It's just that he's untestable right now...you see, he doesn't respond to any verbal cues at all...so we're not real sure at this point. We'll know more as he gets older."

Feeling more and more intimidated by their evasiveness, "You said 'probable.' What about all these other kids you see with autism? Are most of them mentally retarded?"

I realized the doctors must have been trying to soften the blow, but instead were making me even more upset by not giving us concrete answers about all the details.

Looking cornered, Dr. Benge said, "A great percentage of children with autism do score below the range of average intelligence; however, a small number do score in the range of normal intelligence."

"What about these 'splinter skills' you hear about some people with autism having...like 'Rain Man' skills...?"

Dr. Frost said, "That's a common misconception. Only about 5% of people with autism have those types of talents, and when they do, they are very isolated areas of superior functioning rather than being of an overall intelligence."

Dr. Benge went on, "Nowadays, with early intervention services such as First Steps, a great percentage can end up in a regular classroom by the time they go to first grade. It's not like it used to be where all disabled children were isolated in a Special Education room. That's encouraging. Do you all have any other questions?"

Feeling that this was our cue to leave, Gordon and I stood and began to gather our things when Gordon said, "What about this therapy we saw called ABA? It said that it was reported to have good success."

Standing to leave, Dr. Benge said, "We are not allowed to endorse any one method of therapy. All we can say is the standard early intervention services work fairly well."

It sounded to me as if that were some kind of an endorsement in itself. We both were realizing that we were supposed to take our packet and our newly labeled child and leave. They had done their job. We were now on our own.

PART II
The Journey to the Eye of the Storm

Shortly after Ben's second birthday we put a trellis archway in the yard. Ben loved to run back and forth through the archway, tracking it with his eyes.

The professional portrait was taken 2 days after Ben's diagnosis. The only way to keep him on the photographers platform was to give him his travel-sized Magna-Doodle. A smile or eye contact was out of the question.

10

"A voice was heard in Ramah,
Lamentation, weeping, and great mourning,
Rachel weeping for her children,
Refusing to be comforted, because they were no more."
Matthew 2:18 NKJV

I don't remember much about the hour and a half drive back home.

I remember the cell phone ringing a few times and Gordon talking to those who had called to inquire about the evaluation results. I didn't want to talk to anybody. I was already sick of trying to explain things to people.

When we got home, Gordon quickly fed Ben a snack and put him down for a nap.

Standing in the kitchen somewhat in a daze, I noticed Ben's baby book lying on a nearby shelf and realized that I had always taken great pains to record every meaningful event in each of my children's baby books. Every detail from the first tooth to the cute little sayings were painstakingly recorded.

I opened Ben's book and began looking through each page.

"First haircut."

"First steps."

When I reached the page entitled "First Words," it was as if time had stood still. The entry entitled "First Word" said, "March 20, 2001; 10½ months; said 'bye-bye' and waved."

I couldn't recall the last time I heard Ben say "bye-bye" or much of anything else for that matter...other than a few numbers.

The entries for "First Sentence," "First Question," "Difficulties in Pronunciation"...were blank. Realizing that today was probably an important event worth noting, I reluctantly picked up an ink pen and began to write at the bottom of the page...

"April 23, 2002- You were diagnosed with autism..."

Instantly, tears sprang from my eyes and streamed down my cheeks and splattered onto the page, "...at the University of Kentucky" I finished, wondering at the same time if he would ever be able to read and understand what was written on all these pages anyway.

The floodgates now opened and I sobbed. This baby that we waited so long to have.... Gordon came into the kitchen and wrapped his strong arms around me.

With the children scheduled to get off the bus soon, I attempted to pull myself together. I still had to be a mother.

I don't remember what the children said when Gordon broke the news. I was just grateful that Gordon had it in him to do all the explaining and answer all the questions the children had.

I vaguely remember Sarah wrapping her small arms around me, "Don't worry, Mom, I'll take care of him after you're gone. You can count on that."

Amazed that she even had the capacity to think of such a thing, I looked down into her face, choked back the tears, "Thank you, that means a lot to know you'd do that."

Dylan, feeling obligated at this point, chimed in, "Yeah, Mom, me too."

It is not uncommon for parents of newly diagnosed children to unconsciously push friends away. It is important to understand that your friends may also be experiencing feelings of helplessness and may be at a loss for how to best help you.

****

Unfortunately, due to economic constraints, I also had to be a dental hygienist. Having patients scheduled back to back for two solid months and no one else able to see them, I felt obligated to get myself out of bed and go to work. When I arrived the next morning, I came in the back door and as usual walked to the back room to put my lunch box in the refrigerator. When I turned around, Jennifer, Pam, and Michelle were all three standing there.

Reaching to hug me, her eyes filling with tears, Jennifer said, "I'm so sorry, Baby. I can't even begin to imagine what you're going through right now."

Pam and Michelle, both understandably at a loss for words, joined in and made it a group hug as we all stood crying.

The following week being Ben's birthday, the girls informed me that they were coming to my house with their children for a birthday party regardless of how Ben might act and whether I wanted them to or not. They had come to understand that it wasn't because I hadn't wanted to have them over for a party, but that prior to diagnosis I felt self-conscious and intimidated by Ben's behavior in contrast to their children.

The party went as expected with Ben highly agitated by all the noise and activity and having a meltdown in my arms when we sang "Happy Birthday."

Everyone tried to be as helpful and understanding as possible. Even though Ben could care less about having a party, it was the only way the girls knew how to offer their show of support. In spite of Ben's behavior, I was thankful to have friends who cared enough to show that they fully accepted my child, flaws and all.

****

Going right back to work was probably the best thing for me at the time. Being a very small town of just a few thousand, many of the patients that came in over the following days and weeks had already heard that something was amiss with my child. Many of the patients came right out and asked about him. Others were more timid and tried asking in a more discrete way, fearing they might upset me. Oftentimes it was nice to get a new patient who knew nothing about me just to have the opportunity to forget, if only for an hour.

My mood, as well as my willingness to talk, fluctuated like the weather. Other times, it was good to have a caring, interested, familiar face to talk to. Many of these patients I had treated for nearly a decade and knew them like my own family. After all, they were a captive audience, unable to leave my chair for at least an hour. Perhaps it was a relief for them to serve as therapist to me for once rather than having to listen to yet another lecture about the importance of flossing.

It absolutely amazed me how many people knew somebody, or knew somebody who had a second cousin, or knew a neighbor's in-law...who had a child with autism. It seemed as if suddenly nearly everybody knew somebody who knew somebody who had autism.

Some patients who had fairly close experiences with autism gave me great insight in what NOT to do. "That little boy's mama just grieved herself to death! She finally had to go on nerve pills an' it's been, gosh, probably four years since they first found out what was the matter with the little guy. He's just pitiful, just sits in front of the TV all day long watchin' the same thing over an' over."

The home front was a busy place with First Steps therapists coming out to do their assessments and scheduling visits. It was recommended that Ben receive one hour per week each of occupational therapy, speech/language therapy, and developmental intervention to take place in the home as well as 2½ hours per week of structured preschool to take place at the First Steps center.

Gordon and I were thankful that we had already adjusted our work schedules more than a year and a half earlier to accommodate Benjamin's needs. Our calendar was rapidly filling up with appointments, and it was more than enough to keep one person busy all day every day.

It is prudent to find socially acceptable replacements for bizarre, stigmatizing, self-stimulatory behaviors rather than to merely try to extinguish them, as it is likely another unacceptable behavior will appear in the extinguished behavior's place.

Benjamin, meanwhile, was developing a whole new repertoire of interesting activities which we discovered at his evaluation were called self-stimulatory behaviors. Dr. Benge had informed us that Ben had at least four of the total six possible areas of sensory dysfunction, and that he perhaps had even five. This being the first time I had ever heard of such a thing, I was fascinated to realize that these sensory malfunctions were responsible for the majority of Benjamin's unusual behaviors.

Gordon had since gone back to the bookstore and asked the clerk to pull up as many book titles as she could find on the subject of autism and give him a printout so that I could pick and choose which ones to order as we could afford them. Our public library had nothing useful to us.

As I began to read the first of many books, I soon learned that most if not all persons with autism have at least one of the six sensory issues causing the affected sense to be hyperfunctional, hypofunctional, or sometimes even an interesting combination of both. This causes the individual to either avoid such sensory input or to crave it as the case may be, and often results in the multitude of unusual behaviors characteristically associated with autism.

For example, Ben's most dysfunctional sense appeared to be visual. He craved visual input of all kinds and seemed bent on seeking this input through activities such as squinting at the lights, lining up letters, numbers, and objects, running past stationary objects while tracking them with his eyes, clapping his hands in front of his face, staring at bright lights, staring at clocks, etc. We soon realized that Ben's list of visual self-stimulatory activities alone comprised a large part of his daily activities. Those combined with all the other sensory mal-functions, pretty much summed up everything he did.

Often, however, we would notice a change in his odd activities as if he were trading them in for something new and more interesting, and soon figured out that it was because he had simply learned new and better ways to gain the sensory input he so craved.

He had been toe-walking off and on for months (which is a proprioceptive self-stimulatory behavior associated with the sense of oneself moving through space) but had recently traded up to walking or running with his head tipped to one side.

Ben's tactile sense was divided, with the largest part of his body being under-sensitive and his mouth, hands, and the top of his head being over-sensitive. He often would purposely run into people or objects as hard as he could in order to receive tactile input. He would also attempt to sandwich himself between a person and the wall or the back of the chair they were trying to sit in, and then proceed to push against them as hard as he could with his feet. Sometimes he would sit and pinch himself on the legs or bite himself on the arms. This particular behavior disturbed me the most.

He also craved auditory input, only not in the form of functional language. This stimming manifested itself in the form of humming, tapping objects against one another or against the floor or furniture, jargoning, and sometimes screaming.

This list is by no means exhaustive and doesn't begin to address even half of the self-stimulatory behaviors (AKA "stimming") in Ben's routine. Finally understanding the purpose of each behavior did much to help Gordon and I know what to do to soothe him.

Self-stimulatory behavior is to a person with autism what heroin is to a narcotic addict. It's their "fix" so to speak.

His brain was so starved without it that the drive for it consumed his every waking moment. Ben was so wrapped up in his search for sensory input that he was unable to acknowledge anyone or anything in his environment that was not a means to gaining this input. Everyone and everything was merely a tool, a means of gaining that which he craved.

I learned that even "normal" people do a certain degree of low-level self-stimulatory behaviors, such as biting their fingernails, twirling their hair, picking their nose in traffic, even smoking.

Examples of more socially acceptable high-level self-stimulatory behaviors are working jigsaw puzzles, crossword puzzles, listening to music, playing golf, and almost any other type of recreational activity that a person finds relaxing.

The difference in the typical person and persons with autism is the need for sensory input is so great that it deprives the individual of normal functioning.

Temple Grandin, an extraordinary woman with autism, wrote in her first book entitled *Emergence; Labeled Autistic,* "Spinning was another favorite activity. I'd sit on the floor and twirl around. The room spun with me. This self-stimulatory behavior made me feel powerful, in control of things....Whatever the reason, I enjoyed twirling myself around or spinning coins or lids round and round. Intensely preoccupied with the movement of the spinning coins or lid, I saw nothing or heard nothing. People around me were transparent. And no sound intruded on my fixation. It was as if I were deaf...." [1]

Reading Temple Grandin's first two books (her second, *Thinking in Pictures: and Other Reports from My Life with Autism*) [2] were of monumental importance in my understanding of Ben.

I read numerous other books penned by professionals and parents that were extremely helpful. But somehow actually being able to access the mind of a person who was so similar to my son helped me to understand more clearly the actual thought processes behind his behaviors as opposed to only a scientific or observational approach about how to simply control behaviors that they did not completely understand.

Temple describes what she thought and how she felt when she engaged in so many of the same behaviors that Benjamin was now engaging in. Granted, there were some differences with Ben seeming to have a few more sensory issues than Temple, but it set me on the right track to understanding them.

Temple became my inspiration in that being almost as deeply affected as Ben, she, through hard work and perseverance on the part of her mother and herself, was a happy, successful, as well as brilliant member of society.

Today, Temple still recognizes residual autistic traits within herself, but she now controls them instead of them controlling her. She has also re-channeled many of her sensory issues into assets instead of handicaps.

Reading her books gave me hope at a time when all seemed hopeless.

With our schedules as busy as they were, there wasn't any "down time" during the day in order for me to read and research. I read while sitting at traffic lights. I read in the bathroom. I read on my lunch break at work.... Looking back, I realize now that I had to keep my mind busy in order to preserve my sanity. The last thing I needed was time to dwell on the fear and uncertainty that lie within me.

Even though Ben's First Steps therapies were all up and running, I knew there *had* to be something more out there and that what he was receiving simply wasn't going to be enough.

I questioned every person I spoke with who knew a child on the autism spectrum concerning what forms of intervention were being used; and all of them had, or were receiving the same or similar services that Benjamin was receiving.

The older ones had transitioned into the school system and were receiving, by and large, the same supportive services through the school district; and yet, not a single one of the children described to me had made any marked measurable improvements. And no one seemed particularly surprised by this.

Wasn't there some kind of old Chinese proverb about children and rising to expectations? So what happened when no one had an expectation?

Without a miracle, none of these children were going to be able to function independently in society as adults. This was not what I wanted for Benjamin. And I didn't necessarily believe that any of those other parents wanted that either. They just didn't know what else to do. What *could* they do? Securing even a speech therapist in rural eastern Kentucky was in itself a feat.

I became obsessed with finding something that would make a difference. There was no time to sit down and wallow in my misery, as bad as I felt like it. I was not going to just sit back and take the token services that were being handed out. Obviously that wasn't going to work. So I read...and I read...and I read....

11

> "count it all joy when you fall into various trials, knowing that the testing of your faith produces patience."
>
> James 1: 2-3 NKJV

Two weeks after Ben's diagnosis I had a breakdown.

That Tuesday morning the eleven-year-old boy with autism that I had remembered from the last year came in the office with his mother to have a tooth looked at. This was the first *real* person with autism I had seen since this whole ordeal had begun. I was mortified. He was absolutely wild. True, he had been wild last year, but last year hadn't been applicable to me, and I hadn't been watching his every move with the dread of what my child's future might hold.

Although precise statistics are unknown, some sources estimate the divorce rate among parents of children with autism to be greater than 80 percent.

This child was as big as his mother and was behaving in much the same way as Benjamin did now. The mother, looking old beyond her years, simply did the best she could to keep him from dismantling the office.

I felt embarrassed for her, but I soon realized that she no longer appeared to be particularly flustered by such behavior. She seemed to be resigned to the fact that this was her lot in life. Her husband had left her years before, much the same as the majority of the others I had heard about.

After they left, I went silently back to my room. The office was unusually and noticeably quiet as everyone returned to their work.

By lunchtime...I lost it.

As I was cleaning my room after my last morning patient, I broke down into wrenching sobs. Jennifer came to the doorway with a helpless look on her face.

Through my sobs, I lashed out at her, "You just don't understand! You've got your perfectly normal baby! Mine is gone forever! I just can't take it!"

Jennifer approached me and silently wrapped her arms around me.

I went home early that day, struggling to drive through my tears and the weight of the world on my shoulders. My faith was beginning to waiver. Was this what Ben's future held? Was there anything I could do to change it? ANYTHING?

Though relieved to finally have a name for what was wrong with my child, did everyone have to behave as if now that he had been labeled, that was it? It's over? Just take your damaged child and learn to get used to it?

The hope that I had gained through reading Temple Grandin's books seemed like an impossible dream when faced with the negativity that surrounded me now.

****

Gordon and I took Ben to see Dr. Charles for his First Steps physical. Everyone went out of their way to offer their condolences. The receptionist shook her head with pity as we walked past.

I could just hear it now, "Poor little thing! What a waste..."

There was an air of tension in the exam room as Dr. Charles performed Ben's physical.

He was exceptionally thorough that day and seemed to make a point of making light conversation throughout the exam. Towards the end, I gave Dr. Charles a copy of the CHAT, telling him that it might behoove him to make copies and to make it a policy to administer it for each and every eighteen month checkup.

Not wanting to appear judgmental and rationalizing that since Dr. Charles seemed to feel guilty for not listening to our earlier concerns, I thought it probable that Dr. Charles might want to continue to be Ben's regular physician. After all, Dr. Charles was a good doctor.

As we were leaving, I asked Dr. Charles how he would feel about managing Ben's future care or if he would feel more comfortable referring him to a physician who specialized in special needs patients. "Oh, no, that's fine," he said, "nobody out there really knows anything about autism anyway, and I can treat his occasional sore throats and ear infections just as good as the next guy."

I could see from the look on his face that Dr. Charles genuinely meant what he had said in a spirit of good will. I could also see that what I was actually asking had *completely* evaded him. I wasn't asking for someone to treat the occasional runny nose! I was asking for someone to be a partner in seeking out ways to help my child get better, to research new treatments, to offer advice, to keep current on the latest studies!

In examining any autism treatment, the goal is to determine the quality of the evidence that supports the claimed results. Are the examiners unbiased? Was a legitimate scientific method of study used? Is the study able to be replicated with similar results? What are the qualifications of the examiners? Do the examiners have a financial interest in the outcome of the study?

He truly thought that nothing could be done to change the course of my child's future...so why bother! I could now see that we were wasting our time and his. Everything I had tried to convey to him had just blown completely over his head. We thanked him kindly and left.

In the future, Gordon and I still saw Dr. Charles from time to time ourselves for cholesterol checks and seasonal illnesses but made a point not to mention Benjamin. Maybe he eventually figured it out, or maybe not...we'll never know.

****

I'm still not sure which was more unnerving... the group we'll call the "Hopeless and Pitying" or the group that I called "The Invalidators."

The Invalidators were a fairly large camp of well-meaning family members and friends who were quick to inform me that I was blowing all this out of proportion...that this was something Ben was definitely going to grow out of.

After all, didn't I remember being told that I myself hadn't uttered more than two words prior to the age of three? Then suddenly I just began talking in paragraphs!

He just doesn't have anything to say just yet! For Pete's sake, leave the poor kid alone!

One good friend from high school even went so far as to tell me that her friend, who happened to be a psychology resident at the hospital where she worked, had told her that it was absolutely impossible to diagnose a child with autism prior to age three and sometimes even four!

This comment took the cake.

"You go tell your friend that I said she might want to just come spend an hour at my house before she goes making those kinds of blanket statements, and she may even want to rethink her career choice if she doesn't know any more than that!"

Looking back, I realize that my friend was only trying to offer some form of comfort that I happened to translate as an invalidation of the facts as they were.

I felt as if they thought I had just made all this up because I had nothing better to do. I just didn't have enough stress in my life and needed to invent some. This was all just a figment of my imagination.

****

I don't think I actually slept the night I went home from work early; I think I fell into a coma. I awoke the next morning feeling somewhat more centered.

I had tried to think of the things Dana had said to me before about God being in control and realized that the only way I was going to be of any use to Ben was to put it in God's hands.

It was also my responsibility to make use of the gifts and talents that God had so graciously given me in order to help my child.

As someone once said, "God helps those who help themselves."

Above and beyond that was God's domain.

I had to stop thinking of all the "what if's" that were beyond my control and get busy doing that which was in my power to do.

I had sent Gordon back to the bookstore to order my next round of books. These were: Karyn Seroussi's *Unraveling the Mystery of Autism and Pervasive Developmental Disorder; A Mother's Story of Research and Recovery* [3] and Catherine Maurice's *Let Me Hear Your Voice* [4].

I began reading Karyn Seroussi's book first, which was primarily about dietary intervention. I had heard dietary intervention mentioned a time or two and knew that Ben did, in fact, have sensitivities to something, we just didn't know what. The ferocity of the reaction he had at eighteen months was enough to make me wonder if that in itself was somehow related to Ben's autism.

I was a bit skeptical about the whole diet thing, but decided I shouldn't rule anything out at this point without carefully examining all the facts myself. My philosophy was anything short of major tranquilizers or shock therapy was worth checking into.

My child didn't speak and didn't know that I existed. What did I have to lose?

The second book, Catherine Maurice's book, was intimidating to me. Having claimed to "recover" both of her two children with autism using this intense and controversial ABA method, I wondered why no one else was recommending it to me. The book was copyrighted in 1993. If it worked so well, why wasn't it being shouted from the rooftops as being the method of choice?

The book referred to a Dr. Lovaas and a book called *The Me Book* [5]. It just didn't make sense, a 22-year-old book that held the "cure" for autism and nobody knew about it? Hmm...must not really work...after all, Ms. Maurice *had* written under a pseudonym.... And these people are talking about forty hours per week of intensive behavioral modification.

First of all, where was the average person supposed to find the time to operate such a program in their home? Secondly, who could afford it unless they lived in a Manhattan penthouse without a financial care in the world like this lady did?

We were just a middle-class family struggling at times to make ends meet. We lived in rural Kentucky in a 1200 square foot house with one bathroom and had never seen Manhattan. Even if it did really work, we would never be able to afford forty hours per week of therapists without moving into a cardboard box, and I was certain there were no therapists of that nature to be found in our neck of the woods anyway....

There. I had made up my mind without even reading past Chapter 8, thus freeing myself from the obligation of even considering such an outlandishly unreasonable method of therapy. It's science fiction. And even if it were true, it's not financially possible, even if we sold our home.... There was no point in wasting my valuable time reading further.

I decided to go back to reading the diet book for now. As daunting as maintaining a gluten free/casein free diet might sound, it was still less intimidating than Ms. Maurice's proposal. I stuck her book in the stack of half-read, useless books.

In the meantime, my three First Steps therapists were making their one-hour weekly visits. They were not making any headway in reaching Ben.

Stefanie, the occupational therapist, was the first to visit. She proved to be very helpful in the realm of sensory integration and was eager to provide us with as much information as possible. She also brought several items to assist in minimizing Ben's sensory integration issues such as a therapy swing, a weighted blanket, a bear-hug vest, and a mini-trampoline.

She also introduced us to the Wilbarger Brushing Protocol, which was a procedure that required the parents and/or caregivers to systematically brush the child's body in a very precise manner, using a soft brush similar to the type given out by hospital nurseries. The procedure should be done for two to four weeks at a time and around the clock every two to three hours while the child is awake.

The purpose of this bizarre-looking routine is to aid the child in sensory integration and help him become more centered, more mentally organized, and decrease a host of undesirable sensory-related problem behaviors such as aggression and self-injurious activities.

Stefanie was amazed that Gordon and I immediately committed to try the procedure without a second thought. What did we have to lose? We weren't commitment shy, and sticking to a regimen such as that for such a short span of time was certainly not a problem if it would help our child.

Stefanie said she had yet to have a family complete a single two-week regimen. They all said it was just too much to remember and too inconvenient.

I didn't get it! How could parents be so unwilling to do such a small thing to help their own child?

Stefanie and I clicked right away. She was genuinely interested in trying to help make a difference and seemed as equally thankful to have us as clients as we were to have her as a therapist. She said most of the other parents she had worked with expected the therapist to "fix" their child in their one-hour a week sessions and refused, during the remainder of the week, to implement any of the strategies they were shown to help their child.

It reminded me of some of my patients who thought they didn't have to do anything to help themselves maintain their teeth during the six months between checkups.

Current research suggests that children with autism are born with average-sized brains, but then by age two, experience rapid brain growth. By age four, many children with autism have brains the size of a normal twelve-year-old. To date the reasons for this remain a mystery.

Ben, however, didn't click with Stefanie quite as well as I had. In fact, as far as he was concerned, she was a minor nuisance.

Stefanie would follow Ben from room to room attempting to engage him in some way, any small way. If Ben were seated on the floor looking at a book or a puzzle when she sat down next to him, he would either turn his back to her or get up a go elsewhere.

It certainly was not due to a lack of effort on her part. Stefanie was a very high-strung, energetic, boisterous person. She was constantly in his face, picking him up, bouncing him on the therapy ball or mini-tramp, or throwing him into the beanbag chair.

Just listening to her explain something to me in her fast-paced, melodramatic way made me short of breath. How any child could ignore her was beyond me. But she didn't quit trying.

Once in awhile her efforts would pay off, if but for a fleeting moment of eye contact or laughter in response to her constant banter. At least it was something.

The other two therapists, Kathy and Barbara, did not fare even half as well as Stefanie.

Kathy, the speech therapist, was a younger dark-haired woman who was far too soft spoken to even deserve a fleeting glance. Gordon and I tried to explain to her that she needed to be more dramatic and speak more loudly in order to gain Ben's attention. After all, even though Ben resisted contact with Stefanie, he did, in his own off-the-wall way, secretly like her. I could tell by his occasional smirk when Stefanie would put on one of her most outlandish shows in order to gain his attention. Kathy, on the other hand, didn't even rate as a minor nuisance. She may as well have been invisible.

Kathy insisted upon following Ben around the house and quietly commenting on whatever Ben happened to be doing at the time.

"I like the way you pick up your blocks...there are four blocks...see 1, 2, 3, 4..." she would say softly. She reminded me of Mister Rogers. I'm sure this was standard speech and language therapy for the "regular" developmentally delayed child, but it wasn't going to cut the mustard with Ben.

Unfortunately, we were stuck with Kathy since she was the only available speech therapist in our town as well as any of the surrounding towns at the time.

Barbara, the developmental interventionist (or "baby teacher" as I was told), turned out to be an even bigger waste of time. She was a sweet, grandmotherly lady in her late 50's. She had been suffering from some health problems as of late and after the first visit, missed the next two. Then she came for one session, then missed three more. Finally, on her third visit we decided it was probably best to see about having her replaced if possible.

When she arrived that day, she spread out her play quilt on the floor and brought out her blocks and various other toys from her bag. After fifteen minutes or so of trying unsuccessfully to get Ben to come sit on her blanket and engage as she seemed to expect him to, she sighed and said, "Well, I guess I've done all I can do here today. I guess I'll be going...." It was obvious that Barbara was not for us. We contacted First Steps about replacing Barbara.

After three weeks of chasing Ben up and down the hallway and from room to room, an exasperated Stefanie came to me one day, "I can't do anything to help him! He won't be still! All he does is run back and forth! I just don't think we're getting anywhere...."

I could tell that Stefanie had reached her limit and feared she may decide that she didn't want to work with Ben anymore.

I attempted to prod her on, "His job as a child with autism is to ignore you. Your job as a therapist is to find a way to make him stop ignoring you."

Stefanie, speechless, stood looking at me sheepishly.

I really liked her and didn't want to lose her, but I could see that she just wasn't able to reach Ben. But neither was anyone else for that matter. The problems she was experiencing with Ben were the same as his own parents were having. *We* couldn't get his attention either.

Stefanie looked wounded.

Feeling desperate, I asked, "Have you heard about this ABA therapy? I've read a few things that say it works wonders for kids with autism, especially the ones who are really high-tempered and aggressive like Ben."

Stefanie said, "I've heard something about it, but we were told in school that technique was not good because they use aversives and try and force the child into compliance. We were taught that you should NEVER force the child to do anything. I'll admit I don't know much more than that, but it just seems like something I wouldn't want someone to do to my child."

I respected Stefanie's opinions and took seriously what she offered. But Ben was completely unapproachable by even the most skilled therapist...even by his own parents...perhaps I needed to look a little further into this ABA before I completely dismissed it.

Stefanie had done her absolute best and had pooled all of her resources in her attempts to reach Ben. She had now run out of ideas.

Where could we go from here? We HAD to do something. But what?

12

"Now faith is the substance of things hoped for, the evidence of things not seen."   Hebrews 11:1   NKJV

~~~~~~~~~~~~~~~~

Some researchers believe that individuals with autism use their brains in atypical ways: for example, they appear to memorize letters of the alphabet in a region of the brain that normally processes shapes.

~~~~~~~~~~~~~~~~

I continued to read and study every moment I could grab.

In the meantime, Ben continued with his First Steps services but seemed to be resisting every step of the way. Gordon and I were constantly trying to intrude on Ben's private little world and occasionally had a few small successes.

Shortly after the diagnosis, Ben began a new and improved form of self-stimulatory behavior.

He had been perseveringly lining up letters and numbers for quite awhile, but had now added a new twist. After lining up his letters in neat little rows across the rug, he would then pick them up one at a time, search out either Gordon or myself, and hold it up with a questioning expression on his face as if to ask, "What is it?"

The exciting thing about this particular behavior was that he made direct eye contact while he waited for a response. As soon as he was told, "T" or whatever the letter happened to be, he would run back into the living room, climb onto the couch, and proceed to slowly lower the letter over the arm of the couch until he had it level with the edge of the arm of the couch. Then he would release the letter and smile with glee when he heard it go "plink" onto the hardwood floor.

Ben would continue this odd ritual for hours at a time and repeat the process through the entire alphabet, upper as well as lowercase. When he finished, he would pick up all the letters, line them up across the rug, and start all over again.

I knew this was a complex form of stimming, with the lining up and the tracking of the letter to the edge of the couch satisfying a visual need and the "plink" on the hardwood satisfying an auditory need. Even though he wasn't attempting to repeat the names of the letters at the time, I hoped he was learning his letters at least. The best part was that he was actually seeking out human interaction.

Sometimes I would purposely delay giving him an answer just so I could prolong the precious eye contact. He would wait patiently until I gave him an answer, and then turn and leave with a satisfied look in his eyes. I was just happy that this strange little activity made **him** happy and also thankful that it seemed to deter him from the aggressiveness and tantruming that had overtaken our lives.

The only vocabulary that seemed to be increasing was numbers and letters (if that even qualifies as "vocabulary"). By the end of May, Ben was counting to "12" and was actually beginning to repeat the names of some of the letters when he was engaged in his odd little routine.

Soon he began counting objects, stairs, people, etc., and gave everyone a chuckle at Wal-Mart when he rattled off every aisle number and price tag we passed. I found it interesting that a 24-month-old could grasp the concept that numbers were actually symbols that represented an amount of something. I hadn't taught him that.

Often I would find him in the laundry room counting hangers or in the cabinet counting canned foods.

One day, Ben was sitting in a highchair at McDonald's with a pile of french fries on his tray. Every so often, he would look over towards me and say, "11," "7," "4,".... At first I thought he was counting his fries, but then I noticed that he would only say those three numbers. Looking down at his tray, I was shocked to see that he had broken up his french fries and actually formed the numbers themselves! They were very crispy fries, so those were the only three numbers he could manage without having to bend them! How ingenious!

"You are so smart, Baby! That *is* an eleven!"

Ben turned his beautiful face up and looked directly at me with those piercing blue eyes...and smiled. I got goose bumps. Such a beautiful sight! Oh how I yearned to see that expression and hear the word, "Mama"...someday... maybe someday.

I had a ray of hope.

****

Around mid-May, Ben started his one morning per week of preschool, where he participated in group activities with other children with disabilities while being supervised by a speech therapist, a developmental interventionist, and an occupational therapist. Gordon took Ben each week since it was scheduled on Thursday mornings and those were always workdays for me.

I didn't feel too optimistic that this type of set-up would do much for Ben since he was already exposed to groups of same-aged peers at least twice a week at church and appeared to grow agitated and over-stimulated in the presence of more than two other children. But we decided to give it a shot. Most days, Gordon hovered nearby, quietly observing Ben's behavior and making note of how he responded to the other children and the therapists. Gordon kept me informed week by week.

Ben seemed to be responding much as we had anticipated, generally keeping to himself, staying occupied by the various puzzles, especially the ones with the letters and numbers.

Scientists suspect there are distinct subtypes of autism and that the immune system may be a critical factor in at least some of these subtypes.

If a therapist or another child attempted to intrude on his world or if the activity in the room escalated beyond Ben's threshold of tolerance, Ben would resort to a flurry of self-stimulatory behavior, running back and forth tracking objects with his eyes and knocking down anyone who happened to be in the way or jabbering in his unintelligible jargon as loud as possible as if to drown everyone else out.

During this same time, I decided to start Ben on "The Diet" as it was commonly referred to by parents of children with autism. This was the gluten-free/casein-free diet (GF/CF diet) described in many of the books I had been reading, particularly Karen Seroussi's book. In a nutshell, the thought being that the bodies of children with autism have an abnormal metabolism, absorption, and reactivity to the proteins gluten and casein (and often many others as well), which can result in the physiological changes often seen among children with autism (gastrointestinal problems, sleep disturbances, skin rashes, etc.).

It is also postulated that the sensory processing problems that drive the characteristic self-stimulatory behaviors are also affected by this metabolic defect and that all these problems can be greatly reduced or even eliminated by completely removing the offending foods from the child's diet. Preferably one protein at a time should be removed so as to be able to gauge which protein the child has the greatest sensitivity to.

At first I was highly skeptical. It did seem like a lot of people in the autism community had heard of "the diet," and even though I didn't necessarily believe that this diet held "the cure," it certainly might hold some therapeutic value for Benjamin. I did know for sure that Ben had some autoimmune issues as well as a multitude of gastro-intestinal issues and skin rashes. He obviously had some allergies to something.

I had enough knowledge of nutrition to be able to creatively ensure that Ben would receive all the nutrients he needed. I knew the food preparation would take a lot of time and energy.

First, I set about removing all sources of casein (milk protein) from his diet. This included all dairy products as well as the much less obvious products containing whey, sodium caseinate, lactose, etc.

Gordon and I did a lot of label reading and after making several substitutions, found it much easier to just post a diet schedule with foods Ben *could* have as opposed to having to research every food presented. This meant carrying Ben's food with us everywhere we went.

Once we had the diet schedule posted and all offending foods discarded, it really wasn't that bad. It took a day or two for Ben to readily accept soy milk, and he seemed to miss his revered vanilla-custard dessert; otherwise, it wasn't too traumatic.

Everything we had read stated that if improvements were to be seen, they would generally be apparent within two weeks of the elimination if not sooner, and that most parents notice the most obvious improvements after the elimination of gluten rather than the casein. However, casein removal was usually suggested first since it was the simplest and least stressful (for both parent and child) to eliminate.

After about three days of being casein-free, Gordon and I did, in fact, notice a marked decrease in the diarrhea/constipation roller coaster Ben so often had, as well as a decrease in the runny/itchy nose. Ben also seemed to have a slight increase in the frequency and duration of eye contact. However, I remained cautious in my observations for fear that I would simply *wish* I saw behavioral improvements and therefore creating improvement where there was, in fact, none.

We had made a point not to inform the therapists of our dietary experiment in hopes that we could glean some unbiased input about any observable improvements. Stefanie commented towards the end of the first week that Ben seemed to be making more frequent eye contact with her. I remained unsure of whether this was a direct result of the diet or perhaps maybe the brushing we had been administering off and on over the previous weeks.

We were absolutely positive, however, that a marked impact had been made in Ben's digestion and other allergy symptoms.

One could arrive at the conclusion that a reduction in physical discomfort could be directly proportional to a reduction in negative behaviors and inversely proportional to an increase in desirable behavior. We all behave better when our source of discomfort is removed. The behavioral gains seemed very small; but we were thankful for any improvement, regardless of the cause.

After two weeks of being casein-free, we proceeded to the next phase, gluten elimination. This was much more difficult since our entire western diet is consumed with breads, cereals, pastas, breaded foods...you name it...it has some form of gluten.

It takes much tenacity to engineer a balanced diet without gluten or casein, but it is possible. Gordon and I were anticipating a great improvement after gluten removal. We were disappointed when no other improvements occurred. We continued to comb over Ben's diet to make sure we weren't missing hidden sources, but still there were no more improvements.

After much thought, Gordon and I decided to keep Ben on the diet since we had taken so many pains thus far. We also decided to make an appointment with a new immunologist for some formal testing to find out definitively what Ben was allergic to before reincorporating the gluten.

I had since become quite skilled at baking potato flour muffins and frying rice flour pancakes, and Ben had grown accustomed to the changes.

****

Somewhat let down, I continued to pore over all the information I could get my hands on. It was beginning to seem as if I had read everything that was out there, and even much of the new material I was finding was redundant.

We had even implemented the "mega-vitamin" B6/Magnesium program as well as all the other suggested dietary supplements but saw no changes.

As I reached the bottom of my stack of reading material, I once again came across that obnoxious book by Catherine Maurice. Sighing, I decided I might as well finish reading it since that was all that was left. I had seen this ABA method mentioned in passing in several of the other books I had read, but no one else had suggested that the program had "cured" their child. All the other books seemed to refer to it more as a supplemental thing the parents had tried, if they tried it at all. Their primary successes had been from something else like the diet, auditory integration therapy, or a combination of several interventions.

Besides, everything I had read said that all the children in the original studies were subjected to thirty to forty hours per week of this intensive one-on-one program.

Even if I did truly believe that this program worked (and I still wasn't sure that I did), how could we find qualified therapists in our tiny, rural, Kentucky town? I loved my hometown, but we weren't exactly the most progressive in education or diversity.

The nearest place I would be able to find people to help would be at least an hour and a half away, and even then, no matter how hard we tried we could never afford it.

I continued reading the book. The more I read, however, the more I began to connect with the mother. I felt her fear, her denial, her grief, her guilt....

Ms. Maurice also described in detail her initial resistance to the idea of behavioral modification (ABA) and how she exhausted every available avenue in search of an easier, "more humane" method of bringing her daughter back.

In today's economy, an intensive behavioral program can cost as much as $73,000 per year. Affordability and availability of these programs vary enormously from state to state.

Her descriptions of her children, especially her son, so often mirrored the behaviors I saw in Benjamin.

She says, "One day I noticed him running up and down the hall, looking to the side. I followed him. Up and down he ran, looking not straight ahead, but off to one side, tracking the line of the wainscoting rail where it ran along the wall at eye level." [6]

As I read that particular passage, I felt a knot in my stomach. So many times I had helplessly watched Benjamin run up and down the hallway, looking over his shoulder as he went.

Even though we were far removed from her descriptions of their apartment doorman, their trips to France and Spain...there still ran that common thread: the family members who suggested it was all a figment of her imagination, the doctors who held no hope, the sheer desperation of it all....

As many others before had suggested, I too had once doubted whether her children ever truly had autism, or whether it had only been a "mild" case. I no longer doubted.

As I continued to read her story, I began to see myself in her place and realized that her thoughts could have just as easily been my very own. I couldn't put the book down. I *had* to know what happened to her children. I read with great anticipation her accounts of each tiny success. Her joy became my joy, her hope became my hope....

When she described the first time her daughter looked up and said, "Hi... Daddy," [7] I read with such bittersweet joy that I cried. But at the same time that I shared her joy, I felt my own despair.

I believed in her story now. But how is it that God has blessed her family with the means to take action and give her children back, but I have not been blessed with the same? How unfair that my child should become another hopeless statistic due to lack of funds and available therapists!

Our family worked hard to live a Christian life; how could He neglect us so?

...or had He?

After reading two-thirds of the book and carefully studying the descriptions Ms. Maurice made of her children's behavioral programs and how they worked, I made a decision.

I don't have the money, but I have the brains. I have the determination. And most importantly *the God* to do this.

Late that evening after my bath, I came out of the bathroom (my official office where I could read without distraction!) and made an announcement to Gordon.

"I've been thinking..."

Gordon looked up with a feigned look of dread, "Oh no, not again!" he said jokingly.

I sat down in his lap in the recliner and began to describe what I had learned from Catherine Maurice's book and how it was all beginning to make sense to me now.

"I know there's nobody around here to do it and I know we can't afford it...but I KNOW we can figure out how to do it."

Gordon looked over the pages I showed him, his brow furrowed deeply, considering what I was proposing.

Trying to sway him, "Look, there's even a phone number listed where you can call and order the original book written by Dr. Lovaas that tells you step by step how to do it!

"We can take turns working with him...all we can do is try...it can't hurt." I pleaded.

I quickly flipped to the pages where Ms. Maurice described her daughter acknowledging her Daddy.

"See, read this. Can you imagine Ben saying something like that?" I said wistfully.

Gordon looked up, stroked my hair lovingly. "Whatever you think, Baby...we can give it a try."

I knew I had to have him behind me 100%. I couldn't do it alone. Thankful, I hugged him tightly.

That night, I slept more peacefully than I had slept in months. I knew in my heart that I had exhausted every available avenue. I knew in my heart that this book was true. Whether it worked with Benjamin the way it had with her children remained to be seen, but I knew I couldn't live with myself if I didn't at least try.

God IS in control. He has the power, and He helps those who help themselves, and it was now up to us to use what talents we had and trust Him to do the rest.

13

"Therefore do not worry about tomorrow, for tomorrow will worry about its own things. Sufficient for the day is its own trouble."

Matthew 6:34 NKJV

It was now mid-July, just a little less than three months post-diagnosis and I waited anxiously for *The ME Book* to arrive. Everything I had read said that the earlier the Lovaas program was begun, the better the outcome, preferably closer to age two than to age three.

A sense of urgency drove me to make as many preparations as I could while I waited the few days for the book to arrive. After all, Ben was 26 months old...the clock was ticking.

Meanwhile, day to day living had become a misery. Benjamin spent his days either in constant motion, looking over his shoulder as he went, or lying on the floor tantruming.

Any attempt to alter these patterns was met with horrifying resistance. Any attempts to intrude on his little world, to lock his gaze with mine, were not just merely ignored, but were avoided like the plague.

These behaviors had so encompassed our lives that a simple trip to the grocery store was a nightmare. I was becoming accustomed to the incredulous stares of onlookers wagging their heads from side to side.

I had discovered that I could not bring myself to say, "He's *autistic.*"

Somehow those two words together used in reference to *my* child could not pass my lips.

To say "He's *autistic*" had a nauseating effect on me; it just sounded... so institutionally clinical.... I preferred to say, "He *has* autism." In my mind's eye, Ben possessed the autism; the autism did not possess him. Autism was not *who* he was; it was but a small facet of whom he was, even though at this point in time autism *was* our whole family. We ate, slept, and breathed autism. We had to. But I was determined that was going to change. We were going to reign in the beast. It was not going to destroy us.

My smiling little boy was still in there. He had to be. Because not so very long ago he had been just that...*a smiling, happy, little boy....* Anymore, the only time I could see traces of that little boy was when Ben finally collapsed from exhaustion in his crib at night.

Unlike many children with autism, Ben did not have sleep disturbances. He ran, screamed, and tantrumed so much during the day that he practically fell into a coma at night.

Many nights I would stand beside his bed and just gaze at him. He was so beautiful in every way, but nothing could compare to when he was asleep. When sleeping, his face resembled that of an angel. He was at peace. The beast that held such a grip on him during the day had left, momentarily. I longed to reach over and hold his little body in my arms and breathe in the sweet baby-smell that he still possessed. But I knew that if I woke him, the beast would return.

I knew it wasn't Benjamin himself that was the beast; *it* was the autism. And I wasn't going to let it have my baby. It might have him for the moment, but it wasn't going to keep him long. We would prevail.

The Scriptures say, "I can do all things through Christ who strengthens me." Philippians 4:13.

Now all I had to do was keep that fact in the forefront of my mind and get to work.

****

Needless to say, that summer was not pleasant. The kids were feeling the effects of not being able to go and do as much as they were used to. Ben's restricted diet in conjunction with his behavior made going out to eat as a family unit completely out of the question.

Early that year, prior to diagnosis, Gordon and I were able to get our vacations scheduled for the same week in July. We were all looking forward to a trip to Michigan to visit Gordon's family.

As the week approached, I became apprehensive as Ben's behavior became more and more unpredictable and aggressive. I found it hard to imagine traveling thirteen hours one-way with a child who couldn't sit still. I found it hard to imagine sleeping six nights in a strange place with a child who had a major meltdown every time you moved the rug over two feet to the right or left. Maybe we could take all of his toys, bedding, food...he had such a need for sameness.

The third week of July finally arrived, and I had spent the majority of the second week trying to prepare. Gordon and I thought it best to try traveling during the night and planned to head out in the evening, hoping that Ben would soon fall asleep.

Dylan and Sarah were running about the house excitedly chattering about playing in the woods and wading in the creek when they got to Grandma Liske's. I was packing the last of Ben's special food into the cooler when Gordon came in the back door out of breath, "I finally...got everything...loaded. Is that everything?"

He had ended up having to purchase a cargo carrier that strapped to the roof of the vehicle in order to bring everything we needed.

I looked up at him and burst into tears, "I can't go!" I wailed, "I'm sorry...Honey.... I just can't!"

Gordon looked at me totally mystified. Not knowing what to say, he held me in his arms and listened to me as I tried to explain through my sobbing.

"...it's just so far...and I know your family will sit around and look at Ben like he's some kind of zoo specimen...and nobody has called for months to see about him...they probably think he has some kind of mental illness or something...and your mom's not in the best of health...and Ben's just acting so wild... it'll just scare her...he'll probably slam into her and hurt her too...and you know he won't sleep...."

By this time, my makeup was all over his shirt and I grappled for a paper towel to wipe my nose.

"Okay, okay, Baby. It's OKAY. Why didn't you just tell me you felt this way?" Gordon pulled my clinging body away from him to look me in the eye.

"I'll just call Ma and tell her and I'll unload everything. Okay? It's okay."

I was so relieved. Even though we had worked so hard to get everything packed and I did truly love going up to visit, now was just not the time. No one from Gordon's family had seen Benjamin since the advent of all the chaos.

The last time they had seen him he was a happy, laughing, adorable baby. We just had to have more time. We were expecting the book any day now, and we really needed to get started.

It is important to recognize that everyone who is close to you will experience a range of emotions similar to those you first felt when you found out your child had autism. Some will be expressed, others unexpressed. Provide them with all the information they need to better understand the diagnosis; then give them time to come around.

We didn't have time for a vacation; the beast never took a vacation, except maybe when Ben was asleep. The beast seemed to be gaining strength every day.

Gordon began dutifully carrying everything back into the house. He brought in all of Ben's bedding and I tucked Ben in for the night.

Dylan and Sarah came into the room, "What's going on? Why is Pa bringing everything in?"

I knew they would be heartbroken and I tried my best to explain it to them, all the while praying they wouldn't begin to hate their brother.

"We *will* do something special this week, I promise. We can go to a movie, take a day trip somewhere...whatever you want to do...we just aren't in a position to travel right now...okay?"

The kids looked up at my tear-stained face. Even though I knew they wanted to protest, they said, "Okay...."

Trying every way I could think of to compensate I said, "We'll send Grandma Liske a plane ticket to come at Thanksgiving or Christmas...maybe that way too Ben will be doing much better and it won't scare Grandma so bad... you know what I mean?"

Both kids nodded in agreement.

"Yeah, Ben does act pretty scary lately," Dylan said, "especially if Grandma hasn't seen him in so long...that would be bad."

The children seemed to be appeased with that and set off chattering about what they were going to do for the next week now that their plans had changed.

Even though I felt guilty for having to disrupt my children's lives for the sake of their sibling, I didn't have to work hard to put myself in their shoes. I had lived my entire childhood in their shoes.

I was the youngest of six children myself and two of my brothers were disabled. My brother, Dana, was six years older and had been born with spastic cerebral palsy and endured numerous leg surgeries and countless hours of physical therapy. Being the youngest, this was all I had ever known and thought nothing of my brother's awkward gait, only that I was proud that he could walk since the doctors said he probably never would.

My brother proudly tells others to this day that when I was five years old, a neighborhood child rudely asked, "*WHAT* is *WRONG* with your brother!"

I looked calmly back at the boy and said, "Nothing, what's wrong with YOU."

Today, Dana lives entirely independently and works full-time as a 911 dispatcher.

When I was six years old my eldest brother, Randy, then twenty-four, suffered a ruptured aneurysm. After neurosurgery to place a shunt, he remained in the hospital in Nashville for over three months in a deep coma. He wasn't expected to be more than a vegetable, if he survived at all.

I remember hardly seeing my mother for all those months.

I also remember the day Randy came home. Miraculously, he had awakened from his coma and gradually regained all of his motor skills, but had extensive damage to his long and short-term memory.

Randy remained with us for many years, and was a constant playmate and companion to me, particularly because he could not recall how long he had been entertaining me; therefore, I took advantage of him as any seven-year-old would!

Current studies estimate the sibling of a child with autism has approximately a 10% chance of having an ASD as well.

After many years, Randy met a nice woman who fell in love with his dashing good looks, gentle nature, and keen sense of humor. In spite of his handicap, she was more than willing to care for him, and they finally were married and even had a daughter.

Still to this day, Randy has permanent long and short-term memory loss. However, Randy remains the happiest, most contented person I have ever met. Sometimes what one perceives as a handicap can actually be a blessing in disguise....

I always loved my brothers and never felt jealousy or animosity toward them. Even as a child, I knew that I was blessed to have all of my mind and body functioning normally.

I think that I probably had less time with my mother, especially in that she was understandably preoccupied with more important matters. I never remember resenting the extra attention given to my brothers; it seemed only natural to me that they should require more.

I think my father tried to compensate for my mother's frequent absences and did an admirable job keeping us fed and bathed as well as often taking us clothes shopping (he let us pick out whatever we wanted!) much to my mother's shock and horror. He would always let us choose the red patent leather shoes for church. After all, they were so pretty, and he didn't care if they matched anything else we had to wear!

I, as well as my sister closest to me, had more responsibilities than other children our age, but somehow our parents helped us feel we were important and indispensable helpers, and we felt a certain sense of teamwork and pride in the achievements of our siblings.

I remember sitting for hours on my brother Dana's bed many mornings rolling what seemed to be miles and miles of Ace bandages that he had to wear at night after his surgeries. I only recall it as fun, while he, my sister, and I sat busily rolling bandages, joking around, and pestering as only siblings can.

Even though we never acknowledged it, the four eldest children in our family were half-siblings to my sister and me. This too helped me identify with my own children in that Benjamin is their half-sibling. The similarities do not end there, because my brothers and sisters were never anything other than just that to me...they were all my brothers and sisters. Dylan and Sarah felt the same toward their brother, of which I was thankful.

No matter how dysfunctional a family ends up being, children can emerge from the adversity stronger and better for it. I felt my own experience as a child helped lay the foundation for the strength I would need to parent my own special needs child and their siblings.

Siblings can learn to understand their own sense of worth, value their good health, learn to be team players, and learn to sacrifice of themselves for the betterment of the whole. Sure, there would be days when my children felt that life would be so much better if it weren't for Benjamin and his problems; but in the long run, they would be better for it. I knew that from experience, and I was thankful to God for that special insight with which to help my own children.

****

Gordon and I spent most of the week trying to gather those things we might need to begin our home program. The only source we had to glean from was the storyline of Catherine Maurice's book. From the text we knew we needed to set aside an isolated space somewhere in the house that would be free from distraction. The obvious place in most homes would have been Benjamin's own room, but since he and Dylan by necessity were roommates, that idea would not work. I supposed it could have, but Gordon and I felt that the intensity of the program itself was infringement enough on Dylan and Sarah without further complicating things.

With such a small home, the only option was our bedroom. This way the living room and other bedrooms would be open for Dylan and Sarah to move about the house during therapy hours as long as they were quiet. We moved our bed closer to the wall to create a large enough space for a very small work area.

The book also mentioned the need for a child-size desk or table and two child-size chairs, one for the child and one for the therapist. The adult was to be as much at eye level with the child as possible. I had the good fortune of obtaining a small metal desk from one of my patients whose wife happened to be a retired school teacher. She had kept several of the old fashioned school desks in the basement for her grandchildren to play with. They were happy to donate it to our effort.

Catherine Maurice also mentioned her behavioral therapist requested that she draw up a list of behaviors she would like to increase and a list of behaviors she would like to decrease, as well as a list of "reinforcers" or things that would serve as rewards or motivators to her daughter. [8]

These reinforcers could either be primary reinforcers, which meant they were small pieces of cookie, M & M's, or sips of a favorite juice, etc. or they could be social rewards, such as praise, hugs, kisses, etc....**if** the child was motivated by these types of rewards.

Many children must begin with basic primary rewards because they are not receptive to social rewards. However, food and drink reinforcers should be replaced as soon as possible by either social rewards or activity rewards in order to prevent dependence on the food rewards.

I could identify with Catherine Maurice's initial feelings that this "animalistic" operant conditioning applied to one's child seemed so unnatural. How could training a child in much the same way as a trained seal produce normalcy? It would seem that the logical end result would be no more than a robot. However, as I read her story and the way that her children blossomed, I held on to my faith.

14

"for assuredly, I say to you, if you have faith as a
mustard seed, you will say to this mountain, 'Move
from here to there,' and it will move;
and nothing will be impossible for you."
Matthew 17:20   NKJV

Thankfully, *The ME Book* arrived towards the end of the week.

Between brief stints of taking Dylan and Sarah to the various activities we had promised in lieu of our trip to Michigan, I quickly devoured the first nine to ten chapters, at least enough to lay the groundwork for us to get started. I quickly skimmed the later chapters with the intent of coming back to them as we progressed.

From the very first chapter I was struck, actually offended, by the directness of the language used to describe *my* child. Lovaas often referred to the children as "developmentally retarded" and was very explicit in his rationale for his methods.

In the chapter entitled "Managing The Child in Community Settings," Dr. Lovaas matter-of-factly stated, "You are unlikely to return to a restaurant or some other public place if all eyes were glued on you and your child as he screamed, threw food, pulled the tablecloth off the table, and knocked the dishes on the floor the last time you were there. Similarly, you become reluctant to invite other people to your house if you remain fearful that your child might disrupt a dinner party. Even mild behaviors, such as his incessant masturbation in front of your guests during dinner, are likely to seriously inhibit your party mood. You and your child end up being prisoners, so to speak; his misbehavior is your jailer." [9]

At first I was horrified, wounded, and disgusted by his unnecessarily graphic descriptions. Then I realized the truth of what he was trying to convey and the necessity of his directness. Parents of toddlers with autism tend to avoid facing the entirety of our children's futures with autism. Generally, we have not even entertained the idea that our tiny, precious angels will one day be large, strong, adult males (or females as the case may be), capable of mopping up the floor with us if we don't get a handle on them...*NOW!* At 26 months old, Ben was already as tall and strong as a 3½-year-old!

Dr. Lovaas refused to "candy-coat" the inevitable truths.

After much reflection, I realized I ought to be thankful to him for poignantly and permanently planting such a horrifying image of my son behaving in such a way as an adult. It served as a negative reinforcer for me to work as hard as I could to make this program work. We had no time to waste and Dr. Lovaas wasn't wasting any time letting me know what would happen if I decided to give up.

Applied Behavior Analysis derives its roots from the early work of psychologist B.F. Skinner who demonstrated, using animals, that behavior can be drastically altered by systematically repeated drills and reinforcement.

I also learned to regard the "retarded" and "brain-damaged" terminology as common to the time frame in which the book was written. In the twenty-first century we are highly aware of a level of "political correctness" that was not so prevalent at that time.

Dr. Lovaas also made mention of physical aversives and addressed their controversial nature. In the new millennium, physical punishment is all the more controversial. What was once considered routine discipline for typical children is now worthy of imprisonment—imagine how the same would go over with lawmakers when applied to a "handicapped" child today.

Catherine Maurice also addressed this issue in her book and chose to refrain from aversives in her own home program [10]. Dr. Lovaas by no means suggested that physical aversives were a requirement, but that in some cases may be needed in order for the program to be successful. He sited examples of children who became so self-injurious that their very health was in danger, such as the child who hit his elbows so hard against his sides continually so as to rupture his kidneys. [11] Dr. Lovaas primarily recommended physical aversives for those children whose behaviors posed an immediate threat to their survival, but are certainly not required.

I was very pleased by the "user-friendliness" of the book. It was written in such a fashion that most any parent could understand and utilize in order to become an effective therapist for their own child. I'm not sure what I expected, maybe something designed for professionals, in a more technical format. In other words—over my head.

After all, Catherine Maurice had a behavioral therapist working with her daughter; somehow I translated that to mean I needed a behavioral analyst to fully understand what Dr. Lovaas had to say. Nothing could have been further from the truth.

It was and still is my belief, however, that this program would be best operated in the fashion outlined in Dr. Lovaas's book with consultants setting up the program and trained therapists, assistants, and parents taking turns operating the day to day drills. A good system of therapist communication and feedback, complete with checks and balances, is most certainly the ideal situation to ensure the success of a home based ABA program. This is to prevent parent/therapist burnout and provide the child with many opportunities to generalize new behaviors and skills across a wide variety of adults.

However, not all of us can be so fortunate. So does that mean that all parents without resources must resign themselves to face the horrifying dinnertime picture painted by Dr. Lovaas? I believe the obvious answer is "no." I believe that Dr. Lovaas wrote the book in the way he did just so that parents *can* help themselves to whatever degree their financial and geographical restrictions permitted. Just because an arrangement is not ideal does by no means suggest that it will not work or that it is not worthwhile to put forth the effort.

The first unit of the book explained the basic teaching principles, explained how to present instructions to the child, how to break down teaching material into small components, how to select reinforcers (both positive and negative), and how to use them in teaching.

The next unit contained the programs required for getting the child ready to begin learning, such as how to sit in a chair (and stay in it), how to teach attending skills (eye contact and keeping still), and how to manage tantruming, self-stimulating, and other disruptive behaviors.

After reading these units, I realized that I had a hard row to hoe, so to speak, ahead of me. The very idea of Ben ever sitting still in a chair of his own free will seemed ridiculous. The idea of Ben sitting in a chair on command was...well...totally unthinkable! Ben was so entirely unmanageable that ANY demand placed on him was met with the wildest fits of rage, screaming, kicking, head-butting, anything to cause you to remove your demands and allow him to go back into his own little world.

Then I read, "Keep in mind that sometimes it is the child who is particularly aggressive or who looks very bizarre when you make demands of him who will progress well in the program; he is responding." [12]

Well, I certainly prayed we had a case in point here. I had remembered from psychology years before, that screaming and other types of aggression were, in fact, forms of communication; it certainly demonstrated that Ben had an opinion about the way things went. That was far better than lying in a passive heap and not caring.

At least I had some leverage. Since he felt so strongly about very particular things and activities, I could use these as reinforcers to shape his behavior...right?

Gordon and I were making preparation for the inevitable battle that lie ahead, how to break the beast called autism without breaking our child's spirit in the process.

I knew full well from reading Catherine Maurice's descriptions of her daughter's initial resistance that we were in for a full-fledged war. Her daughter was a fairly passive child and even she resisted.

We were fully preparing ourselves for a head-to-head with the beast itself....

"If God is for us, who can be against us?"
Romans 8:31 NKJV

15

Dr. Lovaas had spoken the truth, we were indeed prisoners.

Gordon and I busily finished the final preparations in order to begin our prison break the following week. The bedroom was equipped with the two chairs, a clipboard with a chart to track our progress, a handful of potential motivators, a wind-up timer, and a video camera placed atop the dresser and aimed at the work area.

In the two weeks prior, Gordon and I had also placed advertisements in all the libraries, community colleges, and newspapers in the area giving a very basic description of our program and asking that anyone interested in gaining this type of experience (such as future psychology or special education majors, etc.) to contact us for further information.

We knew our potential pool of prospects was slim to say the least, but knew that any number of hours that we could afford would be a benefit to us all. All we needed was the right personality type and a willingness and capacity to learn.

We would provide the right person with a copy of the program as well as "on the job" training. We would learn together through trial and error and continuously monitor one another through the videotaping of sessions, offer constructive criticism as needed, and learn from one another's successes and failures. The main thing was that everyone would need to be on the same page to ensure consistency.

Children with autism, much like typically developing children, are notorious for discriminating among parents, teachers, therapists, and environments; meaning they learn quickly whose "chain they can pull" and when they can pull it, and whose they cannot. Consistency among team members and learning environments is crucial.

We had many calls, but no one seemed to remotely fit. If they had any intelligence at all, it seemed they lacked the personality type required to get the job done. A quiet person was just not going to work, at least not with Benjamin anyway.

We finally ended up with a woman named Virginia who worked in a group home with adults with various disabilities and was currently paired one-on-one with an adult with autism using a behavioral modification program designed for him by a long distance behaviorist who saw him every few months, updated his curriculum, and left specific instructions for Virginia to follow concerning his current list of targeted behaviors and rewards.

Although she had never done this type of work with a child before, she at least had some idea of how the program worked and was accustomed to following a specific protocol of drills and rewards.

The adults that she normally worked with were severely affected, as well as aggressive, and Virginia looked forward to working with "such a cute little boy." The only concern I had was that Virginia seemed to be a little more low-key than I felt she needed to be. However, she also seemed to be very patient.

After voicing my concerns, Virginia assured me that she could and would be more demanding if we needed her to be.

Since she worked during the day, she agreed to work for two hours every Monday, Wednesday, and Friday evenings. This seemed like a wonderful arrangement in that Gordon could work with him during the day, Virginia some evenings, and me the remaining evenings and weekends.

My three First Steps therapists were still making their weekly one hour visits, all to no avail.

The week prior to beginning our home program, I had an idea. How about asking our First Steps therapists to participate in our program!? In the early stages we would all have to work on sitting and attending skills in order to be able to teach him anything, but later on they could each work exclusively on their particular areas, be it speech, OT, or developmental intervention, all the while using the same format as we were using!

I thought this was a great idea...after all, our therapists were making no headway using the methods currently available to them...what did we have to lose? And we would be gaining another three hours of ABA per week as well as exposing Ben to a total of six different faces in order to enhance his generalization of skills across people.

Surprisingly enough, when I presented my idea to our First Steps primary service coordinator, she actually agreed with me. After all, it was supposed to be an Individualized Family Service Plan, and for the first time that she could recall we as parents were willing to take over the helm and direct the entire group as a team as opposed to sitting helplessly along the sidelines expecting our therapists to fix our child.

We called a meeting to officially revise our service plan and explain our program to our therapists as a group. Our OT, Stefanie, was still somewhat uncertain, but agreed to try anything in light of Ben's current progress to date.

Our new developmental interventionist, Angela, was more gung-ho, being currently enrolled in a graduate class that addressed this type of intervention. She was thrilled to have the opportunity to put into use some of the techniques she had only been able to read about.

I was positive that both Stefanie and Angela possessed the ability as well as the personality to do a wonderful job.

Our speech therapist, Kathy, was another story.

She did not have the personality, nor did she remotely like the idea of a parent telling her how she should do her job. She seemed to enjoy hauling all her little toys in each session and sitting in the floor playing and chattering away in her sing-song voice, all the while oblivious to the fact that Benjamin was totally ignoring her. Not to mention that Ben had yet to acquire any new language other than the occasional utterance that may have remotely sounded like a real word but was never to be heard again. Kathy's delusional idea of "progress" was simply *not* what we had in mind.

After realizing that she was in the minority, Kathy half-heartedly agreed to give it a try. Gordon and I both knew that we would have to keep a close watch in order to prevent Kathy from undermining the program by being too lenient with Ben. We wished there were some way we could replace her, but there still were no other available speech therapists.

We gave each therapist a copy of *The Me Book* and a brief description of how we planned to operate, and then told these women we would see each one the following week.

****

Saturday, July 31, 2002 finally arrived. Gordon and I planned to work together in two hour segments over the weekend in order to be able to work together for the first few sessions. We knew it would take more than one person at the beginning.

We also were able to arrange for Virginia to be with us in order for her to be able to see what we were doing, as well as for Ben to learn to see her as an authority figure from the very beginning.

Dr. Lovaas had explained that we should expect horrible displays of anger at the beginning. He was so very right....

Gordon, Virginia, and I filed down the hallway to the back bedroom with Gordon carrying Ben in his arms.

It was decided that I would be the first to present the drills for the first five minutes, which would be followed by one minute of allowing Ben to jump on the bed, a favorite activity for him.

It is important to remember that when your child acts bizarrely, strikes out at you, or otherwise attempts to frighten you into removing your demands from him, it ultimately only hurts him in the long run. Be strong for your child's sake.

We would rotate therapists over the two hour session, with a longer break for Ben after the first hour.

After closing the door, Gordon placed Ben in a standing position in front of one of the tiny metal chairs. I sat in the other small chair in front of Ben. Gordon sat on his knees behind Ben's chair in order to physically prompt Ben to sit, offer hugs and kisses, or hold him in the chair as the need may arise. Virginia sat off to one side, temporarily in charge of the timer and also responsible for clapping and cheering.

As everyone took their places, Ben looked around the room with a wild expression as if searching for the way of escape. Never once did he make eye contact to petition us for help or seek comfort or explanation.

The tiny room was overcrowded and contained unfamiliar clutter....

The moment we had diligently prepared for had finally arrived....

I felt a combined sense of eager anticipation as well as ominous dread as I sat in this tiny chair facing my precious child who had no clue what was about to happen to his little world.

"Sit down," I said loudly while holding Ben's shoulders in an attempt to steer his gaze toward me.

As expected...no response.

I immediately steered him by the shoulders into the chair behind him. As soon as his little bottom touched the chair, we all enthusiastically clapped and cheered.

"Good sitting!!"

Ben actually looked directly into my eyes with a look of total bewilderment. I knew he had no concept of what the words "sit down" meant. Language meant nothing to him. I could see now in his eyes the utter confusion as to what had just taken place.

Those three to five seconds that he sat in that chair while Gordon, Virginia, and I showered him with praise are permanently etched in my mind. He did not resist, he did not move...he was simply trying to grasp the meaning of what had just happened to him.

For a fleeting moment, I actually thought this might be easier than any of us had initially expected.

I took him by the shoulders, raised him from the chair to a standing position, and presented the next trial*.

Footnote

*Lovaas defines: *Trials start with the teacher's instructions, including any prompts, followed by the child's response or failure to respond, and the teacher's reward or punishment (if any).* **(13)** The discrete trial procedure is to be thought of as a single teaching unit and must be paced correctly with command, prompt, response, and reward as a neat little package with a definite start and a definite end. This helps the child understand the relationship between what has been said to him, his actions, and the consequences.*

"Sit down."

Again, I physically prompted him by guiding him into the chair...we cheered, clapped, patted and kissed him. For an instant, I thought I could see what looked like a smirk form ever so slightly at the corners of Ben's mouth... then it was gone.

He gave Gordon an odd sidelong glance before proceeding to arch his back and throw himself angrily onto the floor. It had suddenly dawned on Ben the purpose of this rude intrusion on his private little world. He did not cry, but he was NOT going to do anything we wanted him to do without a fight.

As Lovaas had directed, Gordon, Virginia, and I totally ignored his display of defiance.

I lifted him from the floor and issued the next command. "Sit down."

This time when I began to physically prompt him, Ben immediately buckled his legs, arched his back, and hung limply by his arms in my grasp.

Gordon reached out and quickly pulled his little body into the chair, wrapping his arms around him to keep him there. Ben's legs kicked angrily, but Gordon held him firmly in the chair while we all smiled, clapped, and enthusiastically cheered.

"Good sitting!"

He was incensed!!

He pushed against Gordon's strong arms with all his might. His small face was flushed with anger, and I could see the little vein in his forehead begin to pop out.

The thought then flashed through my mind that the part of a hurricane that immediately surrounds the eye is the most violent part of the entire storm. All we had to do was break through that wall to reach the calm that lie within the eye of the storm.

After the three to five seconds, Gordon released Ben from his bear hug and he immediately threw himself onto the floor. He lay there for that brief moment with his face against the carpet as if contemplating his next move.

I noticed his ears were fiery red and could hear his rapid breathing. He still had yet to make a sound. Catherine Maurice had described her daughter's cries of fear as she curled into a distraught ball on the floor. **(14)**

Ben was not afraid...he was furious!

I longed to take him in my arms and explain to him why we were doing this to him...that it didn't have to be this way if only he would let us in....

It was this beast called autism that was preventing him from understanding ANYTHING, as well as preventing him from being able to accept my loving arms around him.

This knowledge was the only thing that drove me to take a deep breath, hoist him from the floor, force a smile, and begin the next trial.

Ben struggled to keep from being lifted to a standing position. His legs were like rubber and I strained to hold him up. I could feel his little heart pounding against the palms of my hands. I could smell the sweetness of his baby's breath as he huffed and snorted in my face like a tiny, taunted, Spanish bull.

It was then, when he looked me square in the eye with a look so filled with purposeful rage that I knew we were doing the right thing...that this was going to work!

We were communicating with him! For the first time in his short life, he knew specifically what I was asking him to do! He *knew* I wanted him to sit in that chair. I had penetrated his world and was attempting to drag him into mine! He hadn't been able to make me remove my demands by his ridiculous displays!

And the beast *hated* it.

I knew it was the beast who hated it and not my Benjamin, because a mother knows her child. I *knew* my baby. I knew him from before the beast had taken him.

Just months ago, I had nestled him in my arms while he gazed trustingly into my eyes and sighed with sweet contentment.

I could see a glimmer of my baby in those raging, storm-blue eyes that now stared at me so contemptuously.... I could see his humanity as he was fighting to comprehend why we were doing this to him.

I had caught my first glimpse of the blessed eye of the hurricane....

We relentlessly continued our assault on the beast. I issued several more commands, each time Ben failed to obey. Gordon whisked him into the chair each time and held him tightly. Praise abounded.

Suddenly, almost unexpectedly, Benjamin began to cry.... He half-heartedly slid onto the floor.

DING! The first five eternal minutes were up.

I lifted Ben into my arms and he sobbed into my neck. His body yielded against mine. I felt euphoric...my baby needed me! I stroked his hair...and for the first time in over a year...he did not resist.... Tears of joy welled up into my eyes.

Gordon's gaze met mine as he sat on his knees taking in the moment. He nodded his head knowingly. He too knew our baby was coming home.

16

"Then He arose and rebuked the winds and the sea. And there was a great calm. And the men marveled, saying, 'Who can this be, that even the winds and the sea obey Him?'"

Matthew 8:26-27   NKJV

We had found our way to the eye of the hurricane...the place of serenity within the raging storm.

Some children have mastered basic attending skills in one hour, while others may take months. Once your child has experienced some measure of success, learning tends to become more gratifying for both child and parent.

We had relentlessly forged ahead and prevailed. God had heard our petition and had given us the tools.... "Ask, and it will be given to you; seek, and you will find; knock, and it will be opened to you," Matthew 7:7.

Of course I had no way of knowing just how far, if at all, Ben would progress with the program. But I had hope now...I had witnessed a side of my child that I had thought was lost forever. I felt energized and determined. I had a hunger and a drive to revisit that fleeting moment when Ben looked into my eyes and *understood*. I wanted more. I knew in my heart there had to be more where that came from.

I had faith in my God, and I knew that it didn't matter ultimately how much Ben would improve. I couldn't know that. All we could do was give our 100% to helping our child. I knew that God was in control, and I would gratefully receive every victory, no matter how great or small.

By the end of the first session, Ben was sitting in his seat when asked to do so.

At first he resented our intrusion on his world and had horrific fits of rage interspersed among periods of complete compliance.

It seemed when Ben actually began to enjoy the interaction and positive reinforcement, the beast would remind him, "You are not supposed to be liking this!" and he would momentarily lash out in an attempt to drive us away.

By the end of the weekend, we were all blessedly tired from our labor.

In only two days, Ben was well on his way to mastering the basic attending skills of "Sit down," "Sit up straight," "Hands quiet," and "Look at me." Granted, it had not been without a battle; yet it was surprisingly soon to have the basic attending skills established.

I had tried not to be overly optimistic from the outset and had planned at least two weeks for each attending skill to be considered mastered ("mastered" meaning reliably carried out without prompts roughly 90-95% of the time).

We used various positive reinforcers, always combining them with social reinforcement (hugs, kisses, clapping, and praise). Ben's favorites were his piggy bank, Magna-Doodle®, and puzzles.

At first each correct response (whether prompted or unprompted) was rewarded, for example, with a coin to drop into his bank, time with his Magna-Doodle® for a quick scribble, or given a puzzle piece to put into the puzzle form, etc. After he had achieved some level of consistent success, the reward schedule would be thinned with only unprompted responses rewarded. Finally, only every third, fourth, or fifth correct response was rewarded until the desired behavior was elicited on demand, with the only reward being praise, and then only at random intervals. Eventually both prompts and rewards could be dropped. These steps are known as "shaping."

When we weren't formally "working in the chair," we were working to replicate what Ben had learned across other domains, such as sitting on request in Bible class or at the dinner table, looking at me when I called to him from across a room, as well as responding to requests made by other "teachers" he encountered. This process is called generalization and it is critical to successful and meaningful learning.

Oftentimes, children with autism are taught very successfully in the formal setting and yet are unable to transfer very little, if anything, they have learned outside the teaching environment. This can happen very easily if systematic generalization procedures are not strictly carried out.

Stefanie arrived the following Tuesday for her first session using our new format. I hadn't spoken with her since the previous week and was excited to show her what Ben had learned.

I opened the front door, "Well...?" she said shrugging her shoulders. "So how'd it go?"

I could tell by her expression and tone of voice that she was not expecting much.

"You are never going to believe it! Come in and let me show you!"

Ben was sitting in the middle of the living room floor quietly looking at a book.

"Ben, let's go work!" I said cheerily.

Ben immediately jumped up and ran down the hallway to our bedroom and sat in his new desk.

"I do NOT believe it!" Stefanie exclaimed. "How did you do that?!"

Ben sat expectantly at his desk while I quickly reviewed the commands and rewards we had covered thus far.

We had set up a camcorder on top of the dresser so that we could track Ben's progress and watch for teacher inconsistencies, as well as learn what methods worked and didn't work for each teacher and monitor problem behaviors.

Before leaving the room, I had Ben stand up and asked Stefanie to give her first command.

Ben smiled and sat down in his seat. For an instant I thought I could detect an expression of pride cross his face.

Stefanie was elated.

I felt confident that she would do well with him due to her enthusiasm and the fact that she was already established in his mind as an authority figure. Stefanie worked with him for her allotted hour and emerged with a new attitude toward behavioral therapy.

"I never dreamed I'd see the day when Ben sat in a chair long enough for me to gain his attention. You know, all the criticism I'd heard about ABA made me really skeptical...but all I see here is promise now...we have something to work with! I can't wait to come back next week!"

Ben had tested Stefanie only a few times and then carried on happily. It was as if he needed the security of knowing exactly what was expected of him and exactly where the boundaries were with each person. Stefanie had passed the test.

The plan was for each of the First Steps therapists to work with Ben on basic attending skills until they were well established and then phase in appropriate drills that coincided with each therapist's area of practice.

The developmental interventionist, Angela, was a natural and also did quite well. After the first week or so, Ben would meet Stefanie or Angela at the door with a smile each time they arrived.

The speech therapist, Kathy, was an expected debacle. Her first session and most thereafter were disastrous. Ben refused to obey her commands, whining and tantruming throughout the entire sessions.

At first, I would stay in the room when Kathy was there, sitting inconspicuously off to the side. I would attempt to prompt *her* when to be more forceful and succinct with her commands as well as more immediate and enthusiastic with her praise. She refused to budge in her techniques.

Kathy seemed insulted that *a parent* would have the gall to usurp her as the authority over their child's therapy. I even went so far as to offer her the videos of Stefanie and Angela's successful sessions in order to prove to her that the technique did, in fact, work and that Ben's resistance was to her mediocrity instead of the program itself as she chose to believe. She simply could not fathom that a child might crave structure, consistency, and a distinct set of rules.

It amazed me that Ben had the capacity to discriminate between teachers so early on in the program. For months, Ben had totally ignored all three therapists, yet now from week one of ABA, he already knew who cared enough to set boundaries and enforce them.

Time-out techniques are often ineffective in many children with autism, simply due to the fact that many children with ASD prefer to be left alone. Therefore, time-out can provide a welcome escape and can in turn cause an increase in undesirable behavior.

I decided after that to leave Ben and Kathy alone together and let them fight it out. My intervening was a waste of time. I could only hope that either Ben would eventually grow tired of bucking her or she would grow tired of resisting me. It truly appeared that he was breaking the rules with Kathy not because he didn't want to learn, but rather because he wanted her to know he preferred his structured routine.

At the beginning, Angela's session immediately followed Kathy's and true to form Ben would fight for an hour with Kathy and then work well for an hour with Angela. However, it seemed that it took 10-15 minutes for Ben to attend well after being with Kathy. We soon decided that Ben would get the most out of Angela's sessions if they preceded Kathy's rather than followed.

I reasoned that one scheduled hour of bad behavior out of an entire week probably wouldn't hurt him and perhaps he could vent some pent up energy and frustrations on Kathy instead of on the rest of us! After all, everyone needs somebody to vent to from time to time.

Kathy stubbornly persevered, refusing to complain since she knew what the answer would be. It seemed such a great loss, as Ben's greatest deficits were in the areas of speech and language. But I felt confident in the rest of our team to more than adequately compensate for what was being lost in a speech therapist. Not the ideal situation, but it was all we had to work with at the time. Ben, by and large, consistently saved his worst temper tantrums just for Kathy. Since she was such a willing scapegoat, we let her deal with it.

"And not only that, but we also glory in tribulations, knowing that tribulation produces perseverance; and perseverance, character; and character, hope."
Romans 5:3-4 NKJV

17

Just like a hurricane, the calmness within Ben lie within the eye.

When I had composed a list of possible rewards with which to entice Ben, it wasn't until a week or so into the program that I realized the majority of items and activities that were most riveting to Ben were those of a visual nature. His eyes were certainly the window to his little soul...in more ways than one.

It now made perfect sense to me, in order to capture Ben's attention I had to provide him with a steady flow of his "fix." After all, he did spend the majority of his waking hours earnestly in search of visual sensory input.

What's the fastest way to make friends with a cocaine addict? Provide him with a steady supply of his preferred drug, of course. Not only will he become your best friend, he will reliably seek you out as long as you are able to supply him with that which his body requires. As distasteful it may be to think of one's child as a drug addict, the analogy holds very true.

All of us as humans are "addicts" of something. That's the reason we get out of bed every morning and do the things we do. To obtain. Are we driven to serve God, others, or self? Are we pursuing peace, power, or prestige? Or basic needs of food, shelter and safety? These answers are complex and multi-faceted, dependent upon the age and capacity of the person. But whatever the answer, we are all a slave to something. If we were not, we would have no desire to live.

I suppose it all goes back to Sigmund Freud's psychoanalytic theories concerning the id, the ego, and the super-ego. Where each person is situated on Maslow's pyramid of self-actualization is relative to the many factors, both internal and external, both concrete and adaptable.

The word "autism" itself is defined as "a mental introversion in which the attention or interest is fastened upon the patient's own ego or a self-centered mental state from which reality tends to be excluded." [15]

In my mind, this is where the rubber meets the road. Is this state of mind strictly internal? Is it concrete? Why would the person who has autism be fastened upon his or her own ego?

Could it be that perhaps the basic, instinctual, primitive needs of the pleasure-pain principle that comprise the id rather than the ego are not being met due to the extent of the sensory integration dysfunctions that drive autistic behavior?

Most children with autism tend to look at the mouth or another part of the face rather than the eyes of someone who is speaking.

It being theorized that the development of the ego is dependent upon satisfaction of the id for basic survival needs, how could a person with autism progress beyond the id when his nervous system continually screamed for that which it needed to prevent it from shutting down? It appeared to me that a person with significant sensory integration problems obviously was searching for a basic survival need, not a mere ego boost.

I had no way of knowing *why* the sensory processing center of Ben's brain could not be satiated in the typical manner of daily life. All I could know for sure was that it wasn't. It made sense to me that if I could find a way to give Ben's brain that which it needed, he could move beyond his continual fight for basic survival and proceed to the next level of development. Right? I was seeing so clearly now that we had the power to manipulate this basic survival need in order to help him move ahead.

Up until now, Ben had violently and effectively, mind you, protected the power to feed his brain that which it needed. The only problem being his methods were socially inappropriate and lacked practical function, thus keeping him "spinning his wheels" and maintaining his isolation in the world. What more could one expect from a two-year-old?

Through behavior analysis we could take control of this critical factor. One must look at their child and realize that *every* behavior serves a function; this is true of all people, with or without a disability. The goal is to discover through observation what that function is, what factors drive it, and what consequences increase or decrease the behavior. This is a functional analysis.

When I observed Ben, 90-95% of his behaviors were driven by the need for sensory input. Obviously, this was something he had to have. Obviously, all other areas of his development were stagnant since so much time and energy were spent in search of sensory input.

Ben had an addicted brain and much like a patient in a methadone clinic needed to have his addiction effectively addressed and regulated before he could proceed with the process of healing and growing.

****

The weeks flew by quickly and once again the splendor of autumn was upon us. Gordon and I were so busy we hardly noticed.

Dylan and Sarah were excited about the new school year and preoccupied with the socializing and the latest fashion must-haves associated with middle school. They seemed to be adjusting to our new way of life and taking it, for the most part, in good stride.

Ben was getting better and better each day. Every morning and evening I thanked God for answering our prayers. Every glance, every smile, every laugh was a blessed gift from above.

Ben had an unusual air of peacefulness and cooperation after each therapy session. He seemed more centered and spent less time in search of intense levels of sensory input. Granted, it was short lived, with some degree of tantruming and stereotypic autistic behaviors filtering back in within an hour or two after therapy had ended. It didn't matter how short the respite was, we were thankful and encouraged by it and hoped that it was a precursor to the more lasting improvements we so anxiously anticipated.

Gaining control of the beast was by no means a simple task, with each new target skill carefully planned and systematically shaped.

Some days it seemed Ben just could not, or would not as the case may be, grasp what was being taught, and we had to return to the think-tank to troubleshoot the crisis at hand. Somehow, we always seemed to be able to develop a new approach; and just when we thought it hopeless, Ben's "light bulb" would suddenly come on.

Sometimes the problem was merely motivational and all that was required was an increase in the frequency or intensity of praise/rewards; other times we simply needed a fresh set of reinforcers to breathe new life into the daily grind. I became very adept at staying one step ahead of Ben and upgrading tasks and rewards before they lost their luster. This was key to maintaining our happy and eager student.

Ben had done fairly well in mastering the basic attending skills, but had to be regularly reminded of them, and periodically praised for maintaining "Good sitting," etc. as he was a very active child, and sitting nicely in a chair for more than five minutes at a time was a huge feat for him. With this in mind, I made sure to incorporate "out of the chair" rewards for good work. For example, after five minutes of work I would allow Ben to turn on his toy keyboard and march around his desk, clapping his hands and stomping his feet in time to the music for thirty seconds.

Scientists have found that there is an excess of white matter in the brains of persons with autism and that local areas tend to be over-connected, while connections between more distant parts of the brain are weak. It was also noted that the brain's right and left hemispheres tend to be poorly linked. The cognitive and behavioral ramifications of these findings are still poorly understood.

This particular activity was one of his personal favorites and a reliably strong motivator for many months. The reason being that it satisfied multiple sensory needs simultaneously: the keys lighting up as they played and the action of watching his hands as he clapped (visual input), the sound of the music and his clapping (auditory input), the movement of marching/bouncing and moving in circles around his desk (vestibular input).

As Ben's confidence grew in his mastery of a skill, the rewards were thinned with only longer periods of hard work heavily rewarded. Ben soon became content with a simple "Great Job!" or "You are so smart!" after correct responses and frequently, performing the skill independently became in itself intrinsically rewarding. This was our goal, shaping positive, socially acceptable behaviors that occurred spontaneously and reliably across all environments.

Stefanie, being an occupational therapist and specializing in sensory integration techniques, was an invaluable resource to me providing new and interesting sensory-rich rewards for Ben. After attending skills were well established, it was a very natural flow for Stefanie to incorporate occupational therapy into the ABA format. The majority of Stefanie's target goals for Ben from the very beginning were sensory related issues with only a few secondary motor issues to deal with.

Stefanie quickly found that having reigned in the power to gain Ben's attention, the sensory integration activities were very simple to address in that the favorites could be utilized as rewards for work on the less than desirable sensory activities. For instance, after spending five minutes sorting different colored play dough balls (the texture totally disgusted him!), he could be rewarded with thirty seconds of bouncing on a huge, nubbly therapy ball.

We followed Dr Lovaas' book* as our basic outline and within weeks my copy became dog-eared and worn as I pored over it day after day, making marginal notes on what worked, what didn't work, and what we added to our curriculum.

Now that Ben could sit quietly for reasonable periods of time and make eye contact on command, our next task was imitation of simple actions. [16] This program was run concurrently with the matching visual stimuli program [17] in order to decrease the monotony of focusing on one single task for days at a time, as well as to help him become more flexible in shifting from one activity to another within a session. (*FOOTNOTE * Please note that the Lovaas book referred to in these chapters was the 1981 edition, *The ME Book* and that the following year, *Teaching Individuals with Developmental Delays; Basic Intervention Techniques* [18] was released as the updated equivalent. It also contains some very helpful additions pertaining to legal issues and obtaining services through the school system.)

In the motor imitation program, Ben was taught, for example, to raise his arms when told, "Do this" while the teacher raised his or her arms. If Ben did not raise his arms, he was physically prompted to do so and immediately rewarded.

We would continue in this way adding different actions each day, taking care that each action was markedly different from the action that preceded it in order to reduce early confusion and frustration. For instance, raising arms was followed by touching nose, and then clapping hands, standing up, etc. Imitation of facial expressions was also included and proved to be great fun for all of us.

Imitation is the primary way young children learn from their environment and is also frequently one of the larger areas of deficiency among children with autism. Teaching this skill opens the door for a multitude of other teaching opportunities for the child, such as learning how to dress and groom himself, how to play appropriately with toys, and the list goes on and on.

As Dr. Lovaas as well as Catherine Maurice had mentioned, Ben had to learn how to learn.

The imitation program also helps pave the way for imitation of language in that the child has been conditioned to believe that when a command has been given, he must at least attempt to imitate or he will be physically prompted to do so; if he doesn't raise his arms, then someone is going to raise them for him. It is helpful to have imitation of actions well established before beginning a language imitation program. Hopefully the child finds true enjoyment in imitating, since it is not possible to physically force a child to imitate language. If he is well motivated to imitate by prior positive experiences, it greatly increases his enthusiasm to learn when the language program is introduced.

After Ben had mastered most of the actions, we began to phase in verbal command only such as saying "Raise arms" while the teacher kept her hands folded in her lap. At first, if Ben did not understand the verbal command without the physical cue, he could be prompted by either helping him raise his arms, tapping his elbows, or giving him a "hint" by the teacher slightly raising her hands from her lap.

We quickly discovered that Ben was a master of sequence memorization, and if great care wasn't taken to deliberately randomize all drills, he would merely memorize the order in which the drills were done. Instead of listening, he would perform the action that he had memorized that should come next.

Dr. Lovaas addresses this problem [19] and also cautions teachers against inadvertently prompting a child with a visual cue in the direction of the correct response. For example, looking expectantly at the child's hands after the command to "Clap hands" has been issued. This causes the verbal command to become obsolete as the child comes to rely on facial cues as opposed to verbal.

Even as Ben had much to learn, so did we as teachers and therapists. We spent many hours examining our techniques, critiquing one another as well as ourselves, learning from our mistakes, brainstorming, and all in all growing right along with Ben.

PART III
The Beauty Within

Sarah, Dylan, and Benjamin, Christmas 2002,
seven months after diagnosis.

18

"Blessed are the meek, For they shall inherit the earth."
Matthew 5:5 NKJV

Around mid-September, Ben was ready to begin the verbal imitation program.

I felt both excitement and apprehension. Part of me felt that Ben had done so well thus far that there was no reason he wouldn't do well with this particular program.

I had made a point to let the First Steps therapists know that I did not want them to teach Ben sign language as they customarily did with children with autism. I felt strongly that Ben had the physical capacity to speak; he had spoken in the past. Even now he jabbered off and on in his unintelligible jargon that to me was evidence that he could learn language. I did not want to provide him with any communication tools that would prevent him from opening his mouth and at least attempting to speak until all hope was lost.

Another part of me feared that our good luck may have run out. I had read about and spoken with so many parents and relatives of children with autism who were non-verbal. Some had even done quite well in other areas and were able to communicate to some degree through picture exchange systems or signing, but I wanted more....

I longed to hear Ben say, "Mama," and to point and ask for the nine-thousandth time in one day, "What dat?" like other two-year-olds.

I had taken so much joy (and occasional stress) from the constant chattering and banter of Dylan and Sarah when they were small. Oh, out of the mouths of babes they say! I had been interrogated with every question from "Who made God?" to "Why did the dinosaurs die?" It seemed that Dylan especially talked 24/7; he even talked in his sleep. More than once I had jokingly threatened to change my name from "Mama" to "Fred." Dylan would often breathlessly say, "Mama, Mama, Mama...hey, Mama, where are we going, Mama?"

Gordon and I still laugh about the endless "Bill Cosby"-worthy discourses of verbally precocious Dylan. Six-year-old Dylan once cornered the visiting preacher at the door and said, "You know, you have a really big cavity in your front tooth right there. You really should do somethin' about that. Do you drink a lot of soda pop? You know you really shouldn't. You know, my Mama could help you with that cavity. Lots of people from our church come to her office and get their teeth fixed and they could fix that for ya...they really could."

At two years old, Dylan and Sarah had each been very conversational, asking two-word questions and commenting on everything they saw. This is how young children learn from their environment, by exploring, inquiring, and imitating.

Dr. Lovaas' book had stressed numerous times that children with developmental delays simply do not learn from their environment like typical children, thus the reason for the seemingly enormous number of hours per week of one-on-one instruction required for these children to make significant progress.

A typical child spends most of his waking hours either observing the actions and words of others or imitating those actions and words. Our goal was to systematically direct Ben to do the same and to keep him engaged as many waking hours as possible in hopes that he would ultimately begin to imitate others without being prompted to do so.

Except for the sporadic unintelligible jargoning, Ben was still silent for the most part. Occasionally, we would think we could make out a "real" word amongst the jabbering, but were never really certain. I knew that Ben possessed the physical capacity to use verbal language, his vocal cords worked, but could his brain tell his vocal cords to say what he wanted them to say?

Ben's receptive language (understanding of what is said) had grown by leaps and bounds over the past few weeks. He now responded correctly without visual cues to such commands as "touch nose" and "give me cup" and was differentiating quite well between subtle verb changes such as "touch baby," "kiss baby," "hug baby," or "pick up baby."

We had taken great pains to condition Ben to imitate reliably through the physical imitation program. Ben now had it thoroughly engrained in his mind that he must respond to each command or he would be physically prompted to do so. He was responding consistently and also seemed to enjoy therapy more and more as his confidence was building with each small success.

We had also developed an impressive arsenal of positive reinforcements in which Ben was willing to work very hard to obtain. Now if only they would be powerful enough to motivate Ben to *want* to speak.

Dr. Lovaas had described the verbal imitation program as "the most difficult one in the book" [20] and warns beforehand that not all children can learn to speak.

We first had to attempt to increase Ben's vocalizations and bring them under temporal control. Which meant any type of vocalization was lavishly rewarded with "Good talking!" until finally he made the association that "talking" elicited a reward and would "talk" on demand in order to gain either praise or a chance to play with a prized toy.

Gordon and I, as well as the kids, made a concerted effort over the following week to make an exaggerated production each time Ben uttered a sound.

It is estimated that more than half of all children with autism have no useful speech by the age of four.

One afternoon, Sarah and I were waiting in the checkout line at the grocery store and Ben was seated in the front of the cart. Some colorful helium balloons were tied to the checkout post and happened to catch Ben's eye. Gazing upward, Ben smiled, pointed, and babbled, "Gurda, gooda, gurda, GOOODDDAAHH!!"

Instantly, Sarah and I smiled, clapped, and simultaneously exclaimed, "Good TALKING, Ben!!"

Ben smiled widely and clapped his hands with joy as we showered him with praise.

Noticing the odd expressions of the people around us, Sarah elbowed me and whispered under her breath, "Mom, everybody is staring at us like we're crazy!"

The checkout woman gave me a puzzled sideways glance as she reluctantly greeted us, "How'er ya'll today?"

"We're great!" I exclaimed breathlessly.

She nodded, "Great..." all the while keeping her eyes averted as she rang up our groceries.

I suppose I could have given her some kind of explanation. But I had found I no longer cared what others thought and that even when I had offered explanations in the past, people didn't seem to understand.

I had discovered the prevailing Appalachian attitude toward people with disabilities (particularly "mental" disabilities) was, "Bless its little heart...." And I didn't want to hear it anymore.

Since Benjamin's diagnosis, I was amazed by how many acquaintances had told me about their "crazy" relatives who had been banished to institutions across the country. These were acquaintances I had known for years, and had no idea before that they even had a brother or sister.

One patient even shared with me about her son, now twelve, who was in an institution on the other side of the state. She visits him three times a year. I had cleaned her teeth for two years and had only been aware that she had three daughters.

Out of sight, out of mind? Now suddenly they were willing to share their experiences with me? Was this supposed to develop some kind of feeling of kinship between us? Was I supposed to take comfort in the fact that we now shared common ground?

Having a child with a disability usually meant having a child who would draw government assistance for the rest of his life. Sure, they might attend school, go through all the motions, and receive some kind of token diploma. But upon graduation, most would return to their homes and spend the days watching television. If by chance they had the fortitude to work, they usually were reduced to repetitive tasks such as folding pizza boxes or rolling silverware.

I knew this from my brother's experiences. People seemed shocked and horrified when my brother moved to Lexington (by himself!) and got a job as a taxi driver. How dare my mother make that poor, crippled thing work! He should be able to draw enough disability to get by…why on earth would he want to work?!

The doctors had said my brother would never walk, that he would always be in a wheelchair. He not only walked, he walked to his vehicle and drove himself to work! My brother drove that taxi for seven years, became a taxi dispatcher, and then received the offer to become a 911 dispatcher. He earns a great living, owns his own condo, and above all, his life is meaningful and he has reached a goal that was considered unattainable.

That's what I wanted for Benjamin, to reach goals far above those ever imaginable. I no longer had time to listen to stories that did anything less than inspire me to press forward.

****

The moment of truth arrived. I finally felt Benjamin knew what was expected when asked to "talk" and he now was "talking" more and more in order to receive praise from all those around him.

It was now time to begin imitation of specific sounds. I remember the day clearly. Benjamin sat down expectantly in his little desk and gazed at me with eager eyes.

He truly enjoyed therapy sessions for the most part. True, we still had moments and days when we were met with fierce resistance, days when that beast called autism ruled, but they were becoming less and less.

In fact, I had noticed that the beast most often reared its ugly head when there had been a break in the therapy routine, such as over a holiday or when Ben had been sick and had missed a day or two of therapy. It was as if our constant barrage against the beast kept it at bay, and if we let our defenses down for only a moment, it would steal its way back in and attempt to overtake us. Once again, the importance of the continual fight was evident. The idea that a therapist breezing in for an hour a week was an effective "recommended treatment" for autism was becoming more preposterous to me day by day.

This particular day, the beast was gone...or at least asleep.... I smiled and patted Ben's hands lovingly. Leaning forward, I looked into Ben's eyes, "Say 'Ah.'"

I paused, waiting for a response... I knew if he failed to speak there was no way I could *make* him respond...

Ben hesitated for a moment, then grinned, "ah...."

I exploded with praise, "YEH! GOOD JOB!"

Ben clapped his little hands with glee.

I repeated, "Say 'ah.'"

Each time Ben responded promptly and correctly.

Then, "Say 'Mmm.'"

Ben paused, "Mmm...."

My heart pounded with excitement.

"Say 'Mah."

Ben smiled, "Mah...."

"Say 'Ma Ma.'"

Ben looked directly at me, his storm blue eyes dancing, "Mah...Mah... Mama...? Mama!"

I leapt from my chair so suddenly that it startled Ben. I fell to my knees, wrapped my arms around his little body, and wept bittersweet tears of joy.

"But let patience have its perfect work,
that you may be perfect and complete, lacking nothing."
James 1:4   NKJV

19

"Finally! Says "Mama" on September 26, 2002; 28 months old," read the entry in Benjamin's baby book.

The day I had fantasized about and feared would never arrive was finally here. Those painfully blank spaces in Ben's baby book were at last being written upon.... I felt like I was living in a dream that I hoped I would never awaken from.

Within a week, he was saying many of the words he already understood from the receptive language program. Granted, he only used a limited few outside of the formal therapy sessions, but he was generalizing them at a steady rate day by day.

We had developed a routine early on in the receptive program in which we would present a flashcard with a given picture, state what/who the picture was, and give it to Ben for him to place in a row across the floor (*this is an example of an intrinsic reward in that Ben derived visual stimulation and satisfaction from the actual process of "lining up" the cards, thus making the activity intrinsically rewarding as well as educational).

Most children with autism must be taught appropriate and imaginative play skills. Mastery of imitation of simple behaviors is an essential prerequisite for successful acquisition of play skills.

We would then say, "Give me dog."

If Ben did not know which picture was the dog, we would prompt him by either pointing or looking at the correct card. Gradually, we would add more and more cards, until often he was receptively choosing the correct card from a field of thirty or more. We had found that this method worked very well for Ben in that it was so intrinsically rewarding to him.

Now that Ben would actually verbalize each flashcard, he could say the words, line them up, and then give each back on command, thus targeting expressive and receptive skills in one activity. This also helped to ensure that Ben understood the words he was repeating instead of just parroting words.

We continued running other programs concurrently, but focused the bulk of our time on speech and language activities. We quickly discovered new and interesting ways to incorporate speech and language into almost every activity.

For example, we created a "Touch Pantry" to help Ben overcome his sensory issues with touching different textures. This high-tech creation consisted of a large coffee can with masking tape around the rim to cushion the edge and contained a mixture of beans, rice, and pasta.

To entice him to put his hand inside the can, I had buried some of Ben's favorite objects deep within the can. Stefanie would reach inside and pull out a treasure. "Oh! Wow! Look what I found! A yellow letter 'Z'!"

This was more than Ben could stand and was just the thing to lure him into plunging his hand into the coffee can. We also effectively used this letter-hiding trick with play dough, grass, and shaving cream.

"What did you find?" Stefanie would ask. If Ben did not respond, she would whisper the prompt, "An 'E.'"

"'E'..." Ben would say, and Stefanie would immediately praise him for "Good talking!"

When he had successfully removed all the letters and objects from the can and lined them across the desk, Stefanie would reverse the game and tell Ben, "Hide the yellow 'Z.'"

Not only was Stefanie expanding Ben's sensory horizons, she was effectively reinforcing his expressive and receptive language with each drill.

Stefanie had become a firm believer in behavior analysis and had begun implementing the skills she had learned from her experiences with Ben with her other clients as well. She now knew that successful autism treatment required a systematic team approach, with no one therapeutic aspect independent of the other.

Angela, the developmental interventionist, was also using the same tactics in her sessions as she worked to teach Ben age appropriate play skills such as playing with blocks, pretending, and turn-taking games.

From the outset, we had been keeping a log which specified the frequency of Ben's correct, incorrect, and prompted responses as well as the frequency and duration of tantruming and self-stimulatory activity. This had been extremely helpful early on, in that we could keep track of Ben's mastery of each skill and see very easily when it was time to move on.

We now found that we no longer needed a log of *each* response. We were running so many concurrent programs that it became more critical just to know who had covered what and how often. We were so deeply immersed in all the subtle nuances of Ben's development that we no longer needed to graph the statistics in such detail in order to know when a skill had been mastered or when it required more work, and a simple checklist was now adequate.

As Ben's language skills steadily increased, a variety of other stereotypical autistic behaviors also began to emerge.

Ben had begun to exhibit echolalia, which is the repetition, either partial or complete, of sentences that are heard. Echolalia talk occurs not only in children with autism, but also among typical children, but tends to peak around thirty months of age and then steadily drop off. [21]

At first, this was somewhat amusing. I would give Ben a command, such as "Say 'Blue truck.'"

Ben would echo, "Say blue truck...."

Ben also did not understand the concept of answering a question.

Someone in a store might say, "What a cute little boy! Hi there, what's your name?"

"...what's your name?" he would say.

I might whisper a prompt, "Say Ben...."

"Say Ben...."

I quickly learned to stop prefacing verbal prompts with the word "say."

For the most part, Ben exhibited immediate echolalia, which meant that he repeated what he had just heard. Other times, however, he would echo parts of sentences he had heard days earlier (delayed echolalia) such as quotes he had heard on *Sesame Street.* This brought to mind scenes from the movie "Rain Man," where Dustin Hoffman would repeat the entire Abbott and Costello routine of "Who's On First" over and over.

Psychologists still do not fully understand why persons with autism often echo. Some believe it is yet another form of self-stimulatory behavior and that they simply enjoy the matching of their voice to what has been heard, much in the same way as we had run a "put with same" program in which Ben learned to match like objects together.

Whatever the case, Dr Lovaas suggests that echolalia is a good sign and that many children can be taught to move beyond the echoing stage. He also lists programs to assist in overcoming echolalia as well as other types of language pathology if they persist. [22]

Ben also would occasionally use what Dr. Lovaas terms "word salads" [23] in which he would string together nonsense word combinations such as, "bathtub blue elbow church whale...." As unusual as these things were, I was just thankful to hear Ben's say *anything*.

Aside from being difficult to explain to others, I was largely unconcerned by these language pathologies and did not want to do anything to discourage him by harping on proper word usage at this early point in the program.

Ben would often run up to me with twinkling eyes and "tell me" about his day.

"Bear cup milk bye-bye coat...!"

I would make a point to stop whatever I was doing, stoop to his level, and listen intently.

"Really!? Wow, Ben. You are so smart!"

He would grin his priceless gap-toothed grin, sigh with satisfaction, and go "talk" to the next family member.

Dylan or Sarah would often complain when I urged them to respond to him, "But Mom...! He's not sayin' anything! Why do we have to keep answering him when he's talkin' jibberish?! He's buggin' me...."

I would gently remind them that it wasn't so long ago that he didn't even acknowledge their existence and that all attempts at being social should be encouraged.

"Okay...okay...Cool, Ben, that's *really* interesting...."

****

Drawing, painting, and writing can be very intrinsically rewarding activities for some children, as they are visually and tactilely stimulating.

Ben still took great joy in drawing on his Magna-Doodle® and by the first of October was drawing some interesting illustrations as well as many of his numbers.

Even though Ben had slight gross motor delays, Stefanie felt that his fine motor skills were somewhat advanced for his age but was curious as to why Ben only wanted to write and draw on the Magna-Doodle® and refused to use a crayon or marker and paper.

This annoyed me since I would have liked to have kept some of his early drawings for his scrapbook; but I soon realized that since Ben was such a perfectionist, the Magna-Doodle® was the easiest way for him to correct mistakes. Even the slightest stray mark on his Magna-Doodle® masterpiece would prompt an immediate erasing of the screen and he would start all over.

One morning as I was passing through the living room, I happened to look down and notice one of Ben's many Magna-Doodles® laying in the middle of the floor. I did a double-take when I saw the word "COW" scrawled in childish handwriting. Amazed, I bent down and picked it up. Ben was sitting quietly in the floor behind the recliner looking at a picture book. The kids were at school and Gordon was at work.

I walked over to where Ben was sitting and knelt down beside him with the Magna-Doodle® in hand.

"What is it?" I asked, holding the Magna-Doodle® in front of Ben.

Without looking up, Ben echoed, "Wha is it?"

"No Baby, What is it?" I repeated, tapping the Magna-Doodle® with my finger to get his attention.

He glanced at it quickly, "Cow."

He then turned his back to me as if I were a minor annoyance and returned to the business of looking at his book.

Ben could read? No one was going to believe this, I thought; even I could hardly believe it! I didn't know what to do since it was written on the Magna-Doodle®, so I got the camera and took a picture. How many 2 ½-year-olds can write, much less read?!

I immediately called Gordon at work, "You are NEVER going to believe this!"

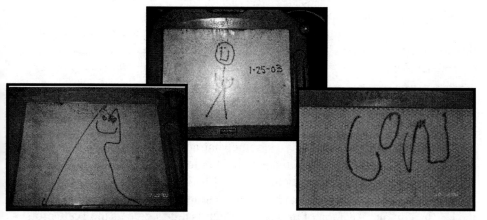

Some of Ben's Magna-Doodle work. The cat was drawn when Ben was 27 months. The stick man at 31 months with date added by Dad. His first word, "cow," was written at 29 months.

20

"Ask, and it will be given to you; seek, and you will find;
knock, and it will be opened to you."

Matthew 7:7   NKJV

In the days that followed, we discovered that Ben could spell more than just the word "cow."

Ben often sat in a corner by himself and silently scribbled on his Magna-Doodle®, or so I had thought he was just scribbling. I now made a point to eavesdrop and found that he could also spell "book," "moon," "ball," and "star."

We had known that he had taught himself to write some letters and numbers but never dreamed he had the capacity to learn to spell. After all, we had been told he had probable cognitive deficits!

A few of the autism books I had read had mentioned some children being able to spell at a very early age. At the time I was quite dubious or at least envious perhaps. Yes, Ben was making steady progress, but he still had huge developmental deficits; I certainly hadn't expected any *advanced* skills to emerge.

I went back to those books and discovered that Ben was exhibiting *hyperlexia*, or the early, precocious ability to decode words. The books didn't spend a lot of time discussing it however, and it was primarily described as just another self-stimulatory behavior. The books all seemed to suggest that even though these children could decode words, they had little, if any, comprehension.

Ben certainly seemed to know what he had spelled. I was sure that Ben had seen the words on TV or in books and had simply memorized the spelling, but he had also made the connection of meaning. He knew he had spelled "cow" and he knew what a cow was.

Early on, I carried about deep within my heart the grief that Ben would always be one of the "low-functioning" kids I had read about. After the initial shock of diagnosis, the reality that Ben's evaluation scores were in the lowest of the low had hit me like a ton of bricks. The doctors didn't give us the evaluation breakdown that day, but said they would mail it within a few weeks. No wonder the doctors were being so evasive when I asked them "how bad is it?"

We had received the "official" evaluation report about two weeks later and it was then that I sat down and looked at Ben's scores on paper. In the speech and language segment, Ben had scored in the first percentile in all domains. In cognitive/social functioning, he scored in the seventh percentile or lower in all domains.... I supposed it was probably a planned thing that the parents weren't given this kind of data on the day of diagnosis; it would have been too much to bear.

The more I read, the more I expected... what? What did I expect? The doctors couldn't tell me what caused autism or much of anything that I could do about it...so why should I expect that they could predict my son's future? Just because they *thought* he had cognitive deficits didn't make it so!

All we knew for a fact was that Ben had autism. This we knew beyond a shadow of a doubt. But that was about it. We knew he had autism, but *no one* knew much else about the hidden dynamics of it.

Perhaps all these persons with autism who were labeled as mentally retarded weren't actually retarded. Perhaps these people just perceived the world in a different way, a way far beyond and above our comprehension. Perhaps testing our children with standardized testing instruments was like giving a visual-perception test to a blind child!

We knew that Ben and all other person's on the spectrum have sensory processing issues that make their world of sensory input something entirely incomprehensible to the rest of us.

But was it a logical assumption that just because some children are more deeply affected than others that they are therefore "low-functioning"?

The books that described "high-functioning" children were describing children who are *more like the rest of us.*

Agonizing over the "correct" diagnosis for your child can prove to be an emotionally and financially draining process when, in general, the more opinions parents seek out, the more confused they become. The specific diagnostic classification rarely alters the recommended intervention. Time and money is better spent addressing the needs of your child... today.

In my mind, the children with more profound sensory processing issues might have the capacity to learn things the rest of us can't. Perhaps they are utilizing more or different parts of their brains than the rest of us...so much so that it interferes with "normal" functioning. But did that mean they couldn't be taught in a method that speaks directly through the sensory channels that drive their bizarre behaviors? Perhaps that was the only way they *could* learn.

Didn't society give accolades to people who think outside the box? Look at Einstein, Mozart, and Picasso. Maybe our kids were just *way outside the box.* So far outside, in fact, that we just didn't get it; and therefore, that which we don't understand is somehow deficient, ignorant, useless....

Since the movie "Rain Man," most people have become familiar with the term "savant." It was interesting to me that "isolated areas of superior functioning" manage to somehow surface spontaneously amidst persons with "profound cognitive deficits." It almost seemed that there was probably more where that came from, only no one had taken the time to cultivate prospective talent and maximize the unique perspective of these "low-functioning" people.

****

October was always my favorite time of year. I loved the brisk mornings, the smell of damp leaves, and the gentle warmth of the afternoons.

This October, however, was different. For one, I was too busy to notice that I even needed a haircut, much less the weather. Secondly, I was on a moment by moment emotional rollercoaster. One minute, I felt full of hope and totally exhilarated by Ben's gains and brainstormed tirelessly in search of creative ways to keep Ben rolling steadily forward. Other times, especially when we were away from our safe haven of structure and comfort, Ben's deficits suddenly appeared painfully enormous in comparison to his neurotypical peers.

How foolish was I to think that we could conquer this beast called autism? How brazen of me to entertain the idea that I had the intellectual capacity to do it myself?

Catherine Maurice had fought a huge enough battle with her team of professionals, a battle so monumental that she even wrote a fascinating book about it. But it appeared that Ben was more severely affected from the outset than her children, and we had also begun our intervention months later than she. Who did I think I was? Was I stupid? Even if I could effect great change by myself, wouldn't someone else have already thought of this idea by now and told the world? Surely many had tried and failed.

But then, when I thought I could sink no further into the depths of hopelessness, Ben would do some small thing and bring my thoughts back to the focus of all this madness.

Ben.

It didn't matter what anyone else had done with their children in the past or what they might do in the future. We had to live for today and try to make change for the better...today.

The big picture didn't matter because the gains that Ben made each day, no matter how they stacked up to the next kid or even Catherine Maurice's kids, only stood to make his future better and brighter...for him.

What I had wished for from the very beginning was a simple blueprint to bring Ben to "normal" functioning. You know, like one of those "*Everything Your Child Should Know by Kindergarten*" books.

Dr. Lovaas's book was a very helpful yet general outline, and I was beginning to realize that there was just so much variability among children with developmental delays that it was going to be largely up to me to figure out exactly *how* Ben could continue to learn.

There were far more factors at play here than just *what* to teach. It seemed every task at hand was a complicated analysis of what made Ben tick and how to mutate the task to make it worthy of Ben's attention.

And who more equipped to do that than his mother? Granted, I might not always understand him, but I had more of the drive and insight to figure it out than anyone else. Just *not* teaching a task that Ben found undesirable was not, in my mind, an option. I had to figure out how to *make* it work.

I couldn't see accepting, "Well, he's minimally verbal and I guess we can't make him talk more if he doesn't want to."

Ben was verbalizing only nouns right now. Yes, he was learning them quickly and seemed sufficiently motivated to use them. But how was I going to move him beyond this? Sure, we had discovered he could spell a few words, but even if he learned to spell and read all the nouns he used, what good would that do?

I had recently ordered a set of picture verb cards from a speech therapy catalog thinking perhaps Ben could learn verbs in this way. He learned a few of them receptively but wasn't particularly motivated by them nor was he verbalizing any of them. I thought about this. What if I were to modify those verb cards so that the word was written on the back?

I had since noticed that all of the words Ben could already spell were from a particular set of flashcards that had the words printed on the back. He seemed reinforced by flipping the card over and looking at the word each time he correctly identified the picture. Obviously, he was reinforced by this activity enough to learn to write the words by himself.

I set out writing the words on the back of each verb card as well as all the other sets of cards that did not already have the words printed on them.

We also began running a program to actively teach Ben to sight read all of the nouns he was already using. My goal was to see how intrinsically motivated he was by this and figure out how I could use any motivation as a tool to produce more language.

I didn't know exactly where I was going with this idea. I hadn't seen a program like this in any of the books I had read and I thought perhaps I may be entirely off track in trying to teach a 2 ½-year-old how to read. I decided it didn't matter.

If Ben was hyperlexic, I felt certain I could find a functional use for it. Just because no on else seemed to find any use for the skill, didn't mean we couldn't.

Ben,
inside his
therapy net
given to him by
Stefanie, the
occupational
therapist.

"You are our Father; We are the clay, and You our Potter;
And all we are the work of Your hand."
Isaiah 64:8   NKJV

21

My intuition was right.

Ben moved quickly through all the verb cards, and having the word on the back was all it took to make the activity intrinsically rewarding.

He also still enjoyed the "lining up" aspect of flashcard drills, so that made the work doubly rewarding for him.

By January, Ben could expressively and receptively sight read over 300 words with comprehension. This was far more than I had anticipated and we continued to add six to ten new words each day.

He quickly mastered reading all the noun and verb cards as well as colors, shapes, numbers, animals, emotions, parts of the body, prepositions, and attributes (big/small, hot/cold, etc.).

Our list of new drills continually grew and mutated as we brainstormed new ways to use what Ben was learning, and I especially focused on ways to promote Ben's spontaneous usage of noun/verb combinations.

One method that seemed especially effective was to place word cards on the desk and prompt Ben to demonstrate what he read. For example "Ben jump," "Throw ball," or "Kiss baby."

As understanding of these concepts grew, Ben began generalizing them to his everyday language. Not only was he responding to what was said to him, he began commenting on his environment.

> *Informal playtime interspersed throughout therapy sessions is important to prevent burn-out and maintain healthy development, both physically and emotionally. A good rule of thumb for young children with autism is 80% work, 20% play.*

One cold and dreary January day, Ben wandered into the kitchen where I stood in front of the stove sampling the pot of chili I had been doctoring.

"Mama eating," Ben stated, looking directly into my eyes for confirmation.

"YES! Yes! Mama IS eating! Good talking, Baby!"

Laying my spoon on the stovetop, I whisked him up into my arms and hugged him tightly.

He put his little arms around my neck and softly patted me in the same way I was patting him.

"I love you..." I whispered softly in his ear.

"I luff you..." he echoed in a whisper.

I had no idea whether he knew what he was saying or merely echoing, but it didn't matter. I knew by the way he yielded in my arms and not only accepted my affection, but reciprocated, that he loved me.

These days, he now eagerly searched my face for approval when he spoke and sought me out for comfort when he was tired or sick.

He needed me!

It was moments like these that made all the hours and hours of reading, thinking, and therapy worthwhile.

God had heard my prayers and had seen fit to answer them.

I knew from the Scriptures that sometimes God's answer to a request is "No" and that sometimes God allows a "thorn in the flesh" to remain with us in order to build our reliance upon Him.

The apostle Paul said that he pleaded with God three times that his "thorn in the flesh" depart from him and that God had said, "My grace is sufficient for you, for My strength is made perfect in weakness," 2 Corinthians 12:8-9.

But I had prayed fervently day after day that if He willed a "thorn in the flesh" that He allow me to bear it in my own body rather than in my child. Wasn't that every mother's prayer?

I knew I could never understand why God allowed some children to suffer and others to thrive, or why sometimes the answer was "No" and sometimes "Yes." In His infinite wisdom, God knows what is best for each of us.

The only comfort we can derive from seeing children suffer and die, or fail to reach what we deem as "quality of life," is knowing that having lost the passing pleasures of this physical life, they have gained the ultimate reward for eternity. What greater gift than that?

God had indeed been answering my prayers over this past year, but in a very graduated, incremental sort of way. There had to be a greater purpose to all of this.

We had certainly learned in a very graphic way about perseverance, patience, teamwork, and what it means to have a faith that works.

We seized every small gift with gladness and thanksgiving.

****

The First Steps therapists were also growing in their faith, in the faith that a determined set of parents can move mountains.

Stefanie and Angela especially seemed to look forward to their weekly visits. Ben would come barreling excitedly through the house to greet them at the sound of the doorbell.

"Hi Stefanie!" he would exclaim with a beautiful infectious grin.

Ben was growing taller and had a perfect, sturdy frame. He was a rough and tumble little boy, but he was still breathtakingly beautiful. And now he was charismatic as well. He had rosy cheeks and enviably long, dark eyelashes that accentuated those unusual eyes that were still the same storm-blue. The only difference now was those eyes were dancing instead of raging.

"Hi Ben! Are you ready to go to work today?" Stefanie would say as she started down the hall toward our bedroom.

Ben would take off galloping toward the bedroom smiling and chirping, "Go work! Go work!"

Stefanie admitted that she loved coming each visit into a home where she knew what her role was to be in the overall scheme of the child's program and the child's parents actually took responsibility for their child's outcome. It simply wasn't reasonable for parents to expect their child to improve by leaps and bounds when Stefanie was only in the home for one hour a week and the parents did little to nothing between visits. She could leave our house knowing that Ben was learning, growing, and generalizing each and every, day and she looked forward to the next week knowing Ben would have made significant progress.

Ben, on his third birthday with Stefanie, the OT. She was always his favorite.

Toward the end of January, I decided to teach Ben phonics in order to increase his word attack skills. He still would only functionally verbalize words that he had a clear picture association for (he echoed other words but did not use them spontaneously).

It became clear that I would have to find another approach to teach more abstract words such as "want," "have," "put," etc., and I thought that phonics might be just the way to accomplish that goal.

Ben grasped the concept of phonics very rapidly with drills such as "What word *starts* with 'mmmm' sound?" We steadily increased the level of difficulty with questions like, "What animal *ends* with the 'ttt' sound?" and began using random rotation throughout.

In language, syntax is the arrangement of words to form grammatically proper sentence structure.

When he could successfully sound out words, I began the program I had in mind. Bizarre as it was, we were teaching our child to talk by teaching him to read first.

I wrote "I want milk, please" on his Magna-Doodle® and placed it in front of him with the command "Read."

I thought this might throw him since all words he had learned to read until now were words he had learned first by picture association. I knew he understood the word "milk," but that was about it. Pronouns also completely evaded him at this point.

Ben gave me a puzzled glance, but proceeded to sound it out.

"I ww-ann-tt milk pp-l-eeea-sse."

I immediately handed him his cup of milk.

He looked momentarily confused, but accepted the cup and took a drink.

I repeated the same procedure.

After four or five repetitions, suddenly Ben's light bulb came on!

"I want milk, please!" he announced proudly as he waited expectantly for the cup that he was now sure would follow.

I then wrote, "I want a kiss, please."

He sounded out the sentence and I instantly planted a kiss on his cheek.

That week, we continued with "I want_____, please" sentences and made certain we now increased our demands on him throughout the day as well.

We would no longer accept only the word "Milk" as an appropriate request and would prompt him accordingly each time until we had successfully shaped full sentences. We continued to expand on this concept in a variety of ways.

In order to teach attributes, I might write "The bowl is cold" and immediately hand him a closed Tupperware bowl with ice water inside. We used the same principle for wet/dry, big/small, soft/hard, rough/smooth, loud/quiet, and the list went on and on.

We also taught prepositions in this manner. "The ball is under the bowl," "The quarter is on top of the block," etc.

Ben's language exploded, and we learned there was no limit to what we could teach him in this manner. Now that he was reading so well, he enjoyed reading story books aloud, and we used these opportunities to give him a good variety of reading material. We took extra care to find books with common age-appropriate social situations that we could attempt to model to help him gain comprehension of the text.

Another adjunctive program that proved to be exceptionally helpful was worksheets. The first few worksheets we designed were basic attribute matching worksheets. For example, he would match, "whisper" to "quiet" or "ice" to "cold." Ben loved the worksheets, and we continually expanded on these in order to increase his generalization from the flashcard format to other, more unpredictable formats. We also made fill-in-the-blank, synonym, opposite, and category worksheets which forced Ben to think for himself and served to further prove his actual reading comprehension.

Critical thinking concepts such as "True & False" were also a true test of Ben's comprehension and generalization of learned concepts with statements such as, "Hitting other boys and girls is good manners" or "Running in the street is safe." This method of teaching proved to be invaluable to me in teaching appropriate social behaviors and personal safety.

Difficulty with pronoun usage, a hallmark speech pathology associated with autism, was finally resolved through our worksheet method using fill-in-the-blank statements such as, "Miss Patty rode _____ bicycle to the store." For some reason, after months of struggling with pronouns, this format caused Ben's light bulb to come on and stay on. However, personal pronoun reversal persisted for many more months before it too was finally resolved. But when he finally "got it," he got it.

Making worksheets kept me very busy, in that I constantly had to shuffle and add new questions to prevent Ben from simply memorizing the worksheet and answering without even reading the question. This was especially true of the True & False worksheets. He would memorize the pattern the first time he did the worksheet.

The amygdala is an area of the brain which plays a role in social behavior. It is now known that this area of the brain tends to be enlarged among individuals with autism. However, the exact correlation between this fact and the social difficulties typically associated with autism remains unclear.

Ben was soon conditioned to come running when he heard the sound of the printer and would stand eagerly waiting, hands outstretched, for his next treasured challenge to finish printing.

We were also able to begin teaching Ben how to ask questions by purchasing "who," "what," "when," "where," and "why" flashcards with written text beneath the picture and with corresponding answer cards. Granted, he learned these all by rote at first, but he began generalizing them as the months went by and I would gradually incorporate these questions into worksheets with subtle changes in the wording to promote generalization as well.

Much to the entire family's relief, going out in public was becoming easier. Everywhere we went we kept a good supply of books, worksheets, and flashcards in the diaper bag to keep Ben occupied. This seemed to help him shut out the extraneous noise and activity in the grocery store or in a restaurant that previously would have sent him into a temper tantrum.

My trick for getting through Wal-Mart on a crowded Saturday was to go straight to the children's book section and grab three or four books for Ben to read as I did my shopping. When I was finished shopping, we just put them back. He seemed to look forward to this routine of new and exciting reading material.

We were an interesting sight to behold as I wheeled my cart up and down the aisles with my 2 ½-year-old who was still in diapers, "Once in a land far, far away there lived a princess...."

Of course, most people did a double-take and many even stopped to ask, "Is he *really* reading that...or is he just pretendin'?"

"Oh, he's really reading alright" I would reply with a hint of pride in my voice.

"And he's *how old*?"   "He's 2 ½."

"You've got to be kiddin' me! Harold, come here and listen to this little baby read!"

Many a checkout person stood with their mouth open as Ben sat in the cart rattling off every brand name as my groceries made their way past him down the conveyor belt. "Fruity Pebbles... Charmin... Nabisco... Heinz Ketchup... Pampers... Tampax..."

I decided it might be a bad idea to enter a public restroom with Ben without first checking the walls for inappropriate graffiti.

I knew this particular reading fixation could probably have been classified as self-stimulatory, but I could also see it served a social purpose. People stopped and spoke to him. Ben soon discovered that it was his reading that drew them to him and would glance up and smirk as they stood making a fuss over him as he read. He actually enjoyed the attention! He was reaching out to others.

Other children at church and school also learned that Ben could read stories to them and would often come and sit beside him and ask him to read to them. He always smiled and gladly obliged.

He had stature in their eyes. He was now a sought after playmate and nothing could have been better for him.

Ben had created a local buzz. News of "The 2-year-old Who Can Read" traveled like wildfire and by mid-February of 2003 the local newspaper had asked to run a feature story about Ben.

For a fleeting moment, I considering declining, realizing that many parents of children with autism chose to keep their child's identity a secret in order to prevent the child from being labeled when they entered school. Others, like Catherine Maurice, chose to protect her children's identities in hopes that they would recover and never know they had autism.

Ben was now gifted in reading, writing, spelling, math, art, and music, as well as an impressive knowledge of rote facts that is stereotypical of many children with autism. I wanted him to grow up to be proud of who he was and where he came from.

Perhaps this was God's plan for us. To give hope to others where there once was no hope. To inspire ordinary parents to believe that ordinary people *can* do extraordinary things. To help others realize that with God's help we can accomplish more than we ever dreamed possible. My son who was lost was now returning to me and I wanted nothing more than to shout it from the rooftops.

The article was an entire page and a half feature, complete with full-color photos, detailing our experiences...and stressing the role of God in our journey.

Within days after the article appeared in the newspaper, the phone began to ring. His Divine purpose for us was becoming more and more clear with each passing day.

22

"For everyone to whom much is given,
from him much will be required..."
Luke 12:48 NKJV

My goal had been to inspire others to greater hope.

I hadn't expected calls from mothers, grandmothers, aunts, even neighbors, asking for all the details of our program.

Many times I would answer the phone and after a hesitation, "...Is this the lady with the little autistic boy?..."

The diversity of each situation was enormous, but the questions were essentially the same. Each time I tried to get some baseline information from the caller about their own situation so I had a feel for their frame of reference. How old was the child? What was his/her level of functioning? What types of interventions had already been done?

The first thing that struck me was how late so many of these children had been diagnosed. This would not have been so surprising had the children been mildly affected; but many of these children had never been verbal, were consumed with stereotypical behaviors, and were not diagnosed until age five.

Whether it could have been considered negligence on the part of the child's physician or whether the parent was in deep denial, in my eyes it was a tragedy. Precious years had been lost.

From day one of our battle with the beast, I had an intuitive sense that I was in a 24/7 race of "Beat the Clock." The doctors had not conveyed that kind of urgency at diagnosis. Sure, they had recommended "early intervention," but had not stressed the need for *intensive* intervention. So what were we supposedly *intervening?* The common cold? Shouldn't the urgency and intensity of the treatment be proportional to the severity and long-term manifestations of the illness if left untreated? Three hours per week of early intervention for a disorder so pervasive as autism seemed as outrageous to me as treating brain cancer with penicillin. Were they hoping for the placebo-effect?

A common thread was all these parents and loved ones *knew* beyond a shadow of a doubt that they were just spinning their wheels and simply being pushed through a system that didn't work. They were just going through the futile motions. And they were left to wonder if even they as parents could see the futility of it all, why didn't the doctors and therapists see? Or did they?

Deep down, I think most parents feel the mainstream medical profession holds no hope for our kids. The interventions that are prescribed are merely a salve to placate parents until the parents themselves realize there *is* no hope... there never was.

Look on the bright side. Now Johnny can sit in a room full of other kids just like him and string beads all day while the classroom aides take turns going outside to smoke. He really enjoys stringing beads now, you know.

The school bus monitor has only caught him masturbating on the bus twice this month and he only smears feces when he gets really bored instead of every day like he used to. He's really made measurable progress in the last ten years.

These were the same types of haunting scenes that Dr. Lovaas had so poignantly described. Scenes that drove me like a mad woman to find a way to spare my child such a future bereft of human dignity if I could possibly help it.

I certainly didn't have all the answers to the mysteries of autism, nor did anyone else for that matter; but in my mind, that was not a call for having *no* hope. I interpreted that as a call *to* hope, a call to find a way to make a difference.

There *are* notable, successful persons with autism. People like Temple Grandin, Stephen Shore, Jerry Newport, and many others. Need they be the exception instead of the rule? Why doesn't mainstream medicine look to these people to find out what they or their parents did right instead of dismissing them as, "Oh, they were just high-functioning to begin with."

Upon further examination, one finds the common thread among all these successful persons with autism is nothing more than *hard work*. Hard work and dedication on the part of themselves, their families, and their teachers. Hard work that never took a vacation until the child ruled the beast instead of the beast ruling the child. There was no magic silver bullet. It was far more complicated than that.

Perhaps this was why funding for research for autism was so difficult to obtain. Pharmaceutical companies had learned a long time ago that pumping exorbitant amounts of money into autism research wasn't doing anything for their bottom line.

Because there *was* no magic pill. And because of that, it didn't pay. Wasn't that the bottom line?

But many parents hopefully asked me, "So what medicines does your son take?"

"He doesn't take any medications."

This response was often met with not only shock, but dismay. So many parents were led to believe that it was impossible to control autistic behaviors without *some* kind of chemotherapeutic intervention.

In my mind, that was the problem. Many people wanted to suppress behavior rather than redirect and reshape behavior. Needless to say, when I tried to explain this concept to many parents, it didn't go over well. Why, their physician had prescribed the medication, didn't they know better than I?

I was floored at the number of chemical cocktails and the subsequent side-effects so many of these children were subjected to, all in the name of hyperactivity, obsessive-compulsiveness, and temper tantrums.

For reasons that remain unknown, children with autism are more likely than other children to have seizures.

"Well, my son is a runner and there's just no way I could make him calm down long enough to teach him anything. You obviously didn't have *that* problem."

Granted, there are instances where medications in the scheme of autism treatment are well warranted. Seizures, extreme self-injurious behaviors, and paralyzing panic attacks come to mind. But in most cases, my belief was they should not be the *first* line of defense, but rather the last.

I genuinely wanted to help other parents, to help other children like Ben. But many of my lengthy phone conversations ended leaving me with a sense of frustration. I could tell by the resignation in many of their voices that this was the last time I would hear from them. I fully understood many parents weren't able to devote the amount of time to a home program that we had been able to devote, but there were many other cost effective ways to rectify the problem if only one took the time to search. Extended family, friends, neighbors, and church members could all be trained to help out. In my mind, if someone wanted and believed in something passionately enough, they *would* find a way—somehow.

Even when I detected this sort of despondency after answering the caller's questions, I would attempt to forge ahead in spite of it, trying to instill in each some seed of hope and determination. I wanted to reach through the phone and shake them and say, "Do you hear what I'm saying! There *is no* easy way! But you can do it! We can find a way!"

In their mind, there had to be an easier way. Had they hoped to pick up the answer to their child's problems at the pharmacy drive-through window and stealthily hide it in the mashed potatoes? They might temporarily mask problem behaviors, but the long-term risks to chemotherapeutic intervention far outweighed the benefits when used as the exclusive source of behavior management.

****

In spite of my growing sense of rejection, there were a few who readily accepted me, in fact, diligently sought me.

One grandmother in particular had kept her eye on Ben each week as he came for his two weekly hours of "therapeutic" preschool where her grandson also attended. She had quietly observed Ben over the preceding months and had taken the opportunity to speak to Gordon as they crossed paths occasionally during drop-off and pick-up.

Her grandson, Jack, was the same age as Ben and they had been diagnosed within weeks of one another. She had overheard the preschool therapists discussing Ben and his progress in our program one day and had inquired of Gordon what it was exactly that we were doing.

Gordon, happy to oblige, gave her our phone number and told her that I was more equipped to explain it than he, saying he only followed my directions and all he knew was that it was working. Such a humble team player!

Ms. Blackwell called me that same evening and shared her grandson's story. Her son and daughter-in-law were still in deep denial. Yes, they admitted Jack had issues, but insisted that since it was "only PDD-NOS*" and *not autism*, that he was going to grow out of it. They took little interest in researching treatment options, staying busy with their older two children and their extra-curricular activities. It was as if they fully expected the problem to go away.

Pervasive Developmental Disorder - Not Otherwise Specified, PDD-NOS - is a form of autism spectrum disorder that meets most, but not all, of the criteria for autistic disorder. Considered by some to be a mild form of autism.

I shared with her all of the interventions we had tried, how we had implemented our home behavioral program, and how we had carefully added to and individualized our program as we went along. I told her I would be happy to help her in any way I could. But first of all she had to convince the parents that they needed help.

Ms. Blackwell knew this and admitted that she had been watching Ben and Jack alongside one another for the past 8 months and had witnessed Ben growing, learning, and blossoming while Jack went progressively backward. Jack's tantruming and self-stimming had grown worse, and he no longer allowed anyone to pick him up. She knew in her heart that what we were doing was working; she had witnessed it with her own eyes. I could hear the desperation in her voice as she held back the tears.

"I just see Jack being pulled further and further away from us every day, and I feel powerless to stop it."

It is not uncommon for parents to remain in denial for months, sometimes even years, following their child's diagnosis.

Ms. Blackwell thought the worst thing for Jack had been the diagnosis of PDD-NOS. So many parents felt since it was *just* PDD-NOS, that things weren't so bad. The reality that a diagnosis of PDD-NOS warranted exactly the same level of intervention as autism seemed to evade parents and professionals alike. And so did the reality that children with PDD-NOS could regress to the point of a diagnostic category of autism if they did not receive adequate intervention. Jack and Ben it seemed had traded places on the autism spectrum.

The most perplexing thing about the situation was *both* of Jack's parents were teachers at one of the local elementary schools. Between them and both of Jack's grandmothers who were willing and eager to help, there was no reason they couldn't set up and operate a program similar to ours.

Our conversation ended that day with Ms. Blackwell resolving to call her daughter-in-law and somehow convince her to call me. She felt that perhaps just speaking to another parent in similar circumstances might bring Jack's problems to the forefront of his mother's mind. Jack's mother had remained totally detached from all aspects of his therapy to this point. She allowed his grandmothers to take and pick him up from preschool as well as be there when the early intervention therapists came.

I agreed to do what I could to make light conversation with Jack's mother and gradually work into a discussion about autism.

Over the weeks that followed, I was able to build a relationship with Jack's mother but she dismissed the idea of ABA with the comment that, "Jack is not as severe as Ben and I just don't think he needs all that."

I continued to talk with her and managed to arrange a "play date" for Ben and Jack one afternoon at her home. Ben proceeded to sit down on the floor beside Jack's four-year-old sister and play nicely alongside her with a dollhouse. He then pretended to drive a toy car across the floor. Towards the end of the hour, Ben and Jack's sister were engaged in a lively game of chase through the house, squealing with pleasure as they took turns being cat and mouse.

All the while, Jack toe-walked back and forth across the living room, screaming, squinting at the rotating ceiling fan, and intermittently smacking his rosy cheeks with his hands.

What language Jack had possessed before seemed to be decreasing daily according to his grandmother, with single word utterances now reserved only for obtaining his basic wants and needs.

Jack's mother was now uncomfortably grappling with the reality of what was before her.

"Jack's grandmother told me about Ben and that he had gotten so much better...if it weren't for that, I'd swear he must have been misdiagnosed."

This was not the last time I was to hear those words.

A week later, Jack's mother called me, "I think we're ready to try whatever it is ya'll do with Ben. Would you be willing to help us?"

I was ecstatic. "Definitely. When would you like to start?"

I gave her instructions on how to choose reinforcers, set up a therapy area, and identify target behaviors. I arranged a time to go over the actual therapy procedures we had employed and recommended they purchase *The ME Book* and read the first unit. I also tried to prepare her for the probable tantruming that would ensue over the first few days or weeks when we tried to gain control of Jack's behavior.

It was a chilly and rainy March morning when I arrived at their home and rang the doorbell.

Jack's grandmother, Ms. Blackwell greeted me at the door with a knowing smile. "Thanks for coming," she whispered under her breath as I entered the house. I knew she was apprehensive about how well this all was going to pan out. She had told me over the phone earlier in the week that Jack's father was rather unenthusiastic about the whole idea.

Now, Jack's parents were joined in an effort to catch him as he ran screaming through the house.

The therapy area was set up just as it should be, in a quiet back bedroom complete with sturdy child-sized table and chairs.

Finally, Jack's father came down the hallway carrying an unhappy Jack over his shoulder. We decided it might be easier to begin the demonstration with one adult at a time in the room. Jack's mother went first.

The command to sit, followed by prompt, and appropriate reward, was met with the expected tantrum. Jack lay on the floor smacking his rosy cheeks as hard as he could and screaming inconsolably.

"Poor Baby!" Jack's mother crooned as she stroked his beautiful blonde curls.

"What should we do now?" she asked.

"Pick him up and do it again," I told her.

She gave me an incredulous look.

I found it difficult to believe that she had read the first unit of Dr. Lovaas' book and wondered how she had survived as a school teacher.

I offered, "Would you like for me to demonstrate for you?"

She reluctantly agreed.

After three rounds of Jack flinging himself from the chair and me calmly picking him up, Jack sat in the chair for a brief moment without instantly throwing himself to the floor. He looked directly at me with an inquisitive gaze. Amidst all the screaming, Jack had shed no tears; he knew that his outlandish behavior had always caused his mother to remove her demands. So who was this lady that wouldn't go away now?

After a few seconds, Jack again flung himself to the floor and resumed his incessant shrieking. Jack's mother could contain herself no longer, and leaping to his rescue, she scooped Jack from the floor. "It's okay, Baby. We're done for today...it's okay."

I couldn't believe it.

"Did you not see when he stopped and looked at me? He was beginning to understand what we were asking of him. You should be expecting some tantruming, that's very normal..." I explained as Jack's mother opened the bedroom door and released him.

He scrambled off down the hallway.

Jack's mother turned to me and said, "I know my mother-in-law said this worked with Ben, but I think Jack is more severe than Ben was. It's not going to work."

I just didn't understand. A few weeks ago, Jack was not severe *enough* to warrant this kind of intervention and now, suddenly, he was *too* severe?

Jack was now prancing about the living room on his tiptoes, happily twirling around like a ballerina as he went.

What was it Jesus had said? No prophet is accepted in his own country?

23

"Take heed that you do not despise one of these little ones, for I say to you that in heaven their angels always see the face of My Father who is in heaven."
Matthew 18:10 NKJV

The splendor of springtime was fully upon us and Ben's third birthday had come and gone marking the end of Ben's state early intervention services. Each of Ben's therapists brought him a gift on their last visit and happily posed with Ben, with tears in their eyes, while we took farewell photos.

It had been just over a year since Ben's diagnosis, a year marked by tears, sweat, and sacrifice; nonetheless, a year of joy, team-work, and blessed victory.

Our entire family had sacrificed greatly. Gordon and I had worked tirelessly, tag-teaming with our jobs, the kids, the chores, therapy, and even sleep. We made every effort to squeeze every drop of value out of every waking moment of Ben's days, as well as try to maintain some semblance of normalcy in the lives of our other children.

Remember to schedule time alone with each of your child's siblings, as well as your spouse, in order to preserve balance and a sense of wellbeing within the family.

They too had made sacrifices. In the past year, spur of the moment excursions had been out of the question, as well as frequent eating-out, and multiple extra-curricular activities.

But complaining had been minimal, and Dylan and Sarah also enjoyed watching Ben blossom day by day. At times, they were in awe of their brother and took pride in bringing their friends over and showcasing Ben's amazing talents. Ben was more than happy to oblige.

"Hey Ben, can you spell armadillo?"

"What's the capital of North Dakota?"

"Can you play 'Mary Had a Little Lamb' on your keyboard for Eddie?"

"See Eddie, I told you my little brother was *that* smart! And he's only three." Dylan would boast, "Pretty cool, huh? And you thought I was making it up!"

Gordon and I continued our home program on our own. We had lost our original helper, Virginia, within one month of beginning the program due to shift changes in her other job and we had since been unable to find anyone else to help. Some, but not all of it was due to a lack of people in the area. We were mostly so busy and focused that we didn't want to waste the time or energy trying to find someone else. Granted, having additional therapists would have been even more helpful to the generalization process, but Ben seemed to be doing quite well with the efforts we made to insist on his compliance with each adult, from Bible class teachers to family friends.

Gordon and I knew Ben was improving by leaps and bounds and were curious to know how Ben would score if he were to be re-evaluated. However, we no longer qualified to have retesting done at the University of Kentucky since Ben was over the age of three and our insurance would not cover the nearly $2,000 cost of re-evaluation.

By September of 2003, Gordon and I had made the decision to move just south of Nashville, Tennessee. After much thought, we had decided the benefits of moving closer to a metropolitan area far outweighed the drawbacks.

A major concern with remaining in eastern Kentucky was the educational options that would be available to us when Ben reached school-age. Ben still had some expressive language lags, but his gifts far outweighed his deficits now and we wanted him to have every imaginable opportunity to excel. I didn't know how we would afford it, but we first had to move to a place where there were more options from which to choose. Educational opportunities for Dylan and Sarah would also be brighter, as both of them were good students and would benefit from the diversity the area had to offer.

Gordon and I were both in professions that could easily be relocated, and within a few weeks, Gordon was granted a transfer, I found a higher-paying position in a dental office, our house sold, and we found another house we could afford. Things had fallen into place so seamlessly; it seemed it was meant to be.

Within a few weeks of the move, we had signed up for our first research study at Vanderbilt, a sleep study of persons with autism spectrum disorders. One of the first phases was an evaluation to confirm a diagnosis of an autism spectrum disorder before beginning the actual study. All of the testing instruments used were different than the original tests given at the University of Kentucky, so I wondered how easily I could compare the two in terms of Ben's overall improvement. Such was to be expected I supposed when dealing with free evaluations, so we weren't complaining.

Ben was happy, cooperative, and quite talkative that day. Afterward, Gordon and I waited nervously while the doctor tabulated the scores.

The doctor finally came into the room, "Wow, comparing these scores with Ben's original evaluation is really quite impressive!" she said with a smile, "Who does your therapy program?"

Gordon and I looked at each other.

"Well, actually *we* do...we always have because we couldn't afford anything else," I explained.

Unsure of what her response would be, I was torn between feelings of pride and shame. After all, she *was* a Ph.D. Who was I, a desperate parent and a dental hygienist of all things, to assume I had the capacity as a behavioral interventionist to impress a doctor at a university known for its excellence in special education?

"I know we don't know exactly what we're doing," I rambled on, "but we really felt like he was getting better...and that's all we could afford...so we brought him here to get some free evaluations and to get some professional guidance to help us out...."

The doctor looked at me with kind eyes, "Stop apologizing! You should be proud of yourselves!"

She smiled at Ben who was busily playing with a toy train he had found in the evaluation room.

"In fact, he barely meets the criteria for this study now. Had he scored one point higher he would have been disqualified. Technically, he is still on the spectrum; but at the age of 3½, and with the kind of work you are doing, he has the potential to not even fall on the spectrum in a few years," she went on.

"His speech and language are now in the low-normal range, his eye contact is within normal limits, he is very socially engaging, and even though this study doesn't call for IQ testing, I can see he falls well within the above-average to superior intelligence range. I can clearly see from residual traits he has in comparison to his starting point, that he is the product of hard work. It's obvious his behaviors have been carefully shaped. He is generalizing well, and I believe his behaviors will become more natural with time."

The moment was surreal.

Please God, I thought, don't let me wake up from this fabulous dream!

"You have reason to go out and celebrate! You have accomplished a feat I have never seen accomplished by parents alone. You've done an amazing

****

In the past year and a half, I had dreamily read over and over the passages in Catherine Maurice's book recounting her daughter's re-evaluation, the tears of joy and the euphoria she and her husband experienced as they drove home afterward. [24]

I had felt pangs of envy and doubt each time I read it. But for some reason I had felt compelled to pull it from the bookshelf every month or so and read it again. I had held on to that hope, just a tiny shred of hope, that just maybe...someday...we too would experience that same joy.

It is not uncommon for children trained using the ABA method to have a robotic or mechanical quality to their patterns of speech. Over time and with practice, this problem can greatly improve or disappear altogether.

Ms. Maurice had overcome this beast called autism not only once, but twice, with her youngest son being diagnosed shortly after her daughter's improvement. But she had a team of competent professionals operating her program and the best doctors money could buy to track her children's progress on a regular basis! We had just muddled along, trusting mostly in our own instincts.

Over the months, I had lamely attempted to track Ben's progress by comparing it to the appendix in the back of Catherine Maurice's book which outlined her son's curriculum over roughly a year and a half span of time. [25] I became obsessed with comparing the skills her son had mastered and at what age, and was driven to make certain that Ben was doing the same. If only we could stay on course with her child, I thought, surely the outcome would be the same!

The ultimate goal was to make our children become indistinguishable from their peers. Wasn't that Catherine Maurice's goal? [26] Was that my goal? Should it be my goal? Or had I only transposed Catherine Maurice's ideal model for her children onto Ben? Actually, the more I thought about it now, that model didn't exactly fit Ben.

In my blind quest to reach the shimmering shores of "normalcy," I had ignored the obvious.

My child was a unique individual. Sure, he shared the common characteristic of autism with her children, as well as the common characteristic of amazing progress. On an academic level, I knew that the similarities should end there.

Foreseeing identical skills between two children with autism made as much sense as foreseeing that your child with diabetes should have the same math skills as your neighbor's child with diabetes. How stupid an expectation was that?

I had obsessively compared Ben's trajectory of development and had tormented myself over every minute detail that did not measure up to my distorted calculations of who and what Ben should become. I was aware that Ben had many skills that Catherine Maurice's children did not, but rather than celebrating and encouraging Ben's gifts, I more often agonized over what I felt he was lacking.

I had presumed that Ben's unique skills were "savant" skills or "splinter" skills, as they are so often called, and in the back of mind feared what I had always heard accompanied these skills. These splinter skills are termed as "isolated areas of superior functioning." The general thought being that persons with splinter skills also possess marked areas of cognitive deficiency, much like Dustin Hoffman's character in the movie "Rain Man."

All the literature I had read said that a low number of children with autism, anywhere from 20-30%, had average intelligence, and the remainder fell in the range of mentally retarded. Persons with Asperger's Syndrome, on the other hand, generally had above average to superior intelligence. At the time of this writing, Ben did not meet the still poorly defined criteria for Asperger's, in that he had severe language delays at the outset and continued to have a slight expressive language delay, both more commonly associated with autism.

Where was the category of individuals with *autism* with all around superior intelligence?

Where was the category of individuals with autism who had moved so far up the spectrum through aggressive intervention that they now constituted a new category?

Catherine Maurice had never described her children as possessing splinter skills. The end result being her children blended nicely with their peers, and for all intents and purposes, were described as "recovered" (some in the autism community are offended by the term). They had reached the point that any residual autistic traits could now be attributable to typical personality variations, [27] such as a penchant for neatness as opposed to an all-out obsession, or a dislike of large crowds as opposed to an incapacitating phobia. They now neatly fell within the parameters of social norms as we know them.

Even though I had set out with a vengeance from the very beginning of this battle determined to prevail and defy the odds, some hidden part of me had believed that "they," whoever "they" are, held the prophecy to what my son could ultimately achieve in life.

So what if he didn't fit into one of the cookie-cutter categories? Who said we couldn't start our own category? Why did I even *need* a category?

Consider Temple Grandin, she didn't fit into any of those classifications now, and she began life in much the same manner as Ben. She rules her autism, and now says she would not want to live life over without it. Autism is the catalyst that has made her who she is today. Granted, it was not without a struggle early on, but it was a struggle that has made her life full and has allowed her to leave a lasting mark on this planet for the benefit of others, both human and beast.

Embracing ones spirituality makes all the difference in overcoming any of life's challenges.

In my mind, autism is a *difference*, just as having red hair, being tall or short, or having dark skin are differences.

Autism was not "the ugly beast" as I had thought of it over the last few years; it was part of who my child *was*. I had thought of it as a beast because I felt helpless to tame it...to contain it. I was frustrated because I didn't understand it. Therefore autism had to be *wrong*...because I didn't understand it? How egotistical was that?! Our children are not a "mistake" of nature, but rather a variation. And just like any other parent, it is our job to teach them in the way that they can learn, which just happens to be different from the way *we* learn.

Ben would *never* be indistinguishable from his peers and the more I thought about it, the more I asked myself, is that what I truly wanted for him? To be like everyone else?

Ben had gifts of thought and perception far beyond the rest of us. He saw this world God created in a different light and we were blessed beyond measure, quite by happenstance, to catch just a glimpse of the treasures that lie within his world. He saw beauty in what others deemed unremarkable and heard music in the ostensibly mundane.

It wasn't *he* that was lacking, but rather *we* who just didn't get it and attempted to exert our standards upon him to a degree; his compliance serving as a window through which he imparts to *us* the intrigue that lies within himself and allowing him to co-exist in a world that views its surroundings so narrowly.

Persons with autism differences are often like strangers in a foreign land; strangers who may live their lives on the outside looking in, sometimes shamefully locked away, punished for their lack of conformity.

I am reminded of an intriguing biblical passage that has drawn much speculation among biblical scholars. The verse appears randomly stuck between two seemingly unrelated verses and says, "Do not forget to entertain strangers, for by so doing some have unwittingly entertained angels," Hebrews 13:2 NKJV

Such a thought provoking statement, a statement placed there most certainly by Divine inspiration for a reason. A reason which demands our attention.

I am not suggesting that parents of children with autism should be satisfied with their child remaining in a state that leaves them unable to function in the world simply for the sake of allowing them to exercise their right to be "different."

We should strive for them to have the best of both worlds, to be able to survive in and make some sense of our world, yet to glory in and maximize their unique vantage point and talents. In this way, all of us can benefit, each party becoming student and each party becoming teacher.

But at the same time, there are those children who, and not for a lack of effort on the part of their parents and teachers, are unable to be "reached." This is where the wisdom and comfort of God has great impact and will give the families of these children the faith to go on, and to have the peace that surpasses all understanding. My belief is that while they may have suffered greatly on this wretched planet, their existence was by no means for naught.

They are the fundamental teachers of humility and contentment, of innocence and true perfection in a world dominated by corruption. Their countenance serves as a window to the consummate beauty of a pure soul on a planet rife with the inevitable ugliness that lies within the human spirit.

I once heard that rearing a child with special needs was comparable to the experience of planning a vacation tour of France and then landing in Holland instead. There are no more available flights to France. You feel frustrated and disconcerted. You had carefully planned your itinerary of when, where, and how you were going to arrive at each landmark along the journey. You realize you need new guidebooks to find your way around and you set about working out a new plan for this unexpected journey. Disappointed, this is not what you had envisioned your journey should be.

You had so dreamed of seeing France...

But then...you begin to notice the breathtaking beauty of the tulips.

Epilogue

"And God shall wipe away every tear from their eyes; there shall
be no more death, nor sorrow, nor crying; and there shall be no more
pain, for the former things have passed away."   Revelation 21:4 NKJV

It is the year 2006, four years since the damning diagnosis.

It is now May, warm and beautiful in middle Tennessee.

I open the curtains in Ben's bedroom and the morning sun comes streaming in.

Ben is six years old now, but still has the face of an angel and like all children, most especially when asleep.

He begins to stir, then sits up in his bed and smiles at me, arms outstretched, "I am *so* glad to see you this morning, Mama."

The eyes are the same storm blue, but the fury of the storm those eyes once held is gone. The gaze is no longer fleeting and distant, but secure and expectant.

"You are? I'm *so* glad to see you too, Baby-Love," I say as he folds his arms around my neck and I swing him down from his bunk bed.

He then dashes off down the stairs to eat breakfast and get ready for school.

Life is good.

I have grown in faith, character, strength, and purpose.

I no longer wander aimlessly through life asking the meaning of it all.

We are born, we live, and we die and somewhere in between, hopefully, we take the opportunity to make a positive impact in the lives of others.

That is what makes life truly meaningful. Not for the glory of self, but for the glory of God, as good stewards of the talents He has given us.

My life has led me places I could have never foreseen because of autism.

We are tourists on a fantastic trip.

A trip that is *nothing* like the one we had intended.

And I've learned that being lost is a frame of mind.

Ironically, I was born without a sense of direction. Zero. I am the person you see wandering through the parking lot looking for her car, the person who gets lost coming back from the restroom in a restaurant. Interestingly enough, I have given birth to this child with some kind of internal navigational device who points and tells me, "Turn west, Mama, we came from that way," as I roam through a department store searching for the exit.

So now, here we are on this journey, without a compass or even a map. We have learned to appreciate the journey itself as they say, instead of the destination. To some, it may seem we have reached a destination of sorts.

To us, it seems the adventure is only beginning, as we now face the challenges of how best to educate our profoundly intelligent child...

And no, we still don't know where we are going, how we plan to get there, or how we are going to afford it. But that's okay. You make the best of where you are at the time and you try to touch the lives of others and be touched by their lives along the way.

We have been asked to share our story in many different venues and I have been encouraged by friends and fellow parents to write this book. I often wondered, "Why the intrigue? What sets us apart from all the other autism success stories?"

There are hundreds of thousands of families who live with autism every day, and each one has a unique and powerful story to share. Why would anyone want to listen to ours any more than the next one?

After talking with parents from every socio-economic and intellectual level, from nearly every continent in the world, I have come to realize the common quandary among us all—fear. By nature, we fear the unknown.

We do not fully understand autism, none of us do. We do not fully understand how to react to it...what to do with it...and ultimately, what will become of our children.

With all these unknown factors, we as parents are overwhelmed, so we naturally look to the professionals to tell us what to do...and then eventually, sooner or later, we figure out the professionals, by no fault of their own, really don't know much more than we do. It's when this realization sets in that the fear can either immobilize us or ignite us. But fear is not the enemy; it's what we decide to do with it that matters.

In the face of autism, none can safely say who will rise to the challenge when we have no clue what weapons to take up, where to go, or what to do when we get there; the ambiguity of it all being not unlike the "War on Terror," where no one is quite certain who is the real enemy and where the battlefield parameters lie.

Sometimes I amuse myself in thinking, "We have found the enemy and they *are us*." Sometimes *we* are our own worst enemy.

Time and time again, parents have come to me saying they just don't have what it takes to help their child. They say they're not smart enough, industrious enough, or strong enough. More often than not, these are people that have far more intelligence, resources, and opportunities than we ever dreamed of having.

And therein lies what defines our story, as well as the reason why, to this day, I have resisted those who have urged me to return to college to become a certified behavior analyst.

I can look that parent squarely in the eye and tell them, "If we can do it, you can do it."

Granted, each child will have a vastly different outcome, but every child, and every parent for that matter, is going to be impacted positively to some degree by the effort.

I don't have a framed piece of paper with any fancy credentials on it other than a birth certificate that says I am the mother of my child. And unlike many parents, we did not have access to anyone other than each other, to guide us along the way, tell us where we had screwed up, or tell us how we might do better.

Many parents go to the ends of the earth and are fortunate to find and fund outstanding, highly-effective programs for their child. But if they do not become involved and *stay* involved, it can all be for naught. I've seen it happen more than once.

No matter what the future holds in advancements for autism treatment, no matter how much money we throw at our child's treatment regimen, no matter if we have the best professionals working with our child around the clock, parents must accept that ultimately the buck stops here with us as parents.

And when we take full ownership of that fact, regardless of how many others are working with our child, we will find then and only then will our child blossom to his or her fullest potential.

That was the mutual ground between Catherine Maurice and myself; we both intimately knew what was going on with our children. Her program, professionally-driven, ours amateurly-driven, but nonetheless, we were *involved every step of the way*.

Her children reached normal functioning and ultimately became indistinguishable from their peers. Our child exceeded any and all expectations to become a National Young Scholar ranking in the 99.9 percentile and has a heartwarming zest for life.

As a true coalminer's daughter with a southern twang to rival Loretta Lynn herself, I was a far cry from the prototype of someone who could develop and implement behavioral programs for a child with autism. I was born and raised in an economically depressed region, and have a propensity for going barefooted and an inborn aversion to all things that require reading directions. I am well aware of my limitations.

My husband is a blue-collar worker with a high school education. He's not the most articulate or creative person, but he's a hard worker with an open mind and a great sense of humor.

An ability to laugh in spite of the circumstances is a must on this journey, as children with autism can be hysterically amusing with their literal and often poignantly, on-target observations about people and life in general. But that's another book...for another day.

We are extraordinarily ordinary. And we had no clue what we were doing.

What if we did something wrong? What if we made things worse? What were we supposed to do next? These are the fears I hear from parents everyday. These are valid fears common to all of us.

But as Ambrose Redmoon once said, "Courage is not the absence of fear, but rather the judgment that something else is more important than fear."

****

I was honored to have the privilege to speak at the Autism Society of America's 2005 national conference. My presentation was entitled *When the Resources Don't Fit; Designing Treatments for Your Child* and I presented alongside two behavior analysts with our group's title being *Parents as Interventionists.*

As I prepared for the conference, I was nervous at the prospect of presenting alongside two behavior analysts, one being a PH.D at that. Would anyone care to listen? Would anyone even show up to hear me speak? Should I try to mask my dialect so people won't think I'm stereotypically ignorant? I had a recurring nightmare that when I stood up at the podium everyone got up and left. Needless to say, my nightmare was not realized; and better yet, the room filled to capacity with standing room only when I approached the podium.

It was a wonderful experience, with my stage fright totally vanishing after the audience's first emotional response to the video footage of Ben's progress beginning from day one. For the remainder of the conference, parent after parent approached me with tears in their eyes. These were parents of children from all levels of functioning and from all walks of life. Many said they had not only left feeling empowered as parents with new strategies they could implement themselves, but they had a renewed sense of hope.

I have never experienced the level of joy and satisfaction as I felt that day.

I also learned from other families who are on the same fantastic voyage. I saw strength, tenacity, and fierceness of love.

But I think I was most inspired by the individuals with autism that I met that day. Watching them interact with one another and hearing as they shared their stories of struggle and success was captivating to me.

They were the guests of honor, and what a fine group they were. Each with their own unique talents, aspirations, and achievements. I was also impressed with the keen sense of humor many of these individuals possessed and was made to laugh on more than one occasion by their dead-on observations concerning the bizarre behavior of the rest of us in the "neurotypical" world, as well as their advice to one another on how to effectively manage *our* behavior.

I continue to speak to groups of parents, physicians, and educators and actively consult with other parents to teach them how to practically help themselves and how to effectively coordinate their child's treatment between home, school, and therapy for maximum impact. I also serve as an advocate, accompanying parents to their child's IEP meetings to assist them in gaining the most from their child's educational experience and to provide moral support as well.

My purpose is strong.

Ben continues to grow and amaze us everyday.

"Typical" six-year-old traits emerge daily it seems, with Ben refusing to play alone, preferring the companionship of others, and following me through the house chattering incessantly.

"Mama, what does the word 'constantly' mean?"

"Is it a synonym for 'always' and the opposite of 'never'?"

"Why do teenagers like to sleep so late?"

"Does Santa Claus ever get lonely at the North Pole?"

"Is heaven north of Detroit or west of Memphis?"

"When I was in your tummy, before I got borned, was I comfortable?"

"Did you know that 1 divided by 8 is 0.125?"

His inquiries concerning the complex and abstract are peppered with the calculated reasoning of genius and yet the sweet innocence of childhood.

He is his own unique individual, with an immeasurable intellectual capacity that has confounded scores of professionals, extraordinarily accentuated by unbridled charm, charisma, and breathtaking good looks.

We had come, somehow, from the deepest depths of fear, sorrow and despair...to this place...confirming the divine fact that it is not within man to comprehend the purpose and power of God.

"Mama, did you know that God lives in my heart *and* in your heart?"

"Yes, Baby-Love, isn't that neat? ...And God has *always been with you*...."

My heart is happy.

My joy is full.

Ben, with some of his artwork at age 3. He was embarrassed by all the attention, but his work hung on display in an exhibit at Vanderbilt's Kennedy Center from April to June 2004.

At age 5 Ben is hamming it up on the keyboard.

Bibliography

(1) Grandin, Temple & Scariano, Margaret M., *Emergence: Labeled Autistic*, Published by Warner Books Editon by Arena Press, a Time Warner Company, Novato, CA., 1986, pp. 18-19.

(2) Grandin, Temple, *Thinking in Pictures: and Other Reports from My Life with Autism,* Published by Vintage Books, a division of Random House, Inc, New York, NY, 1995, originally published in hardcover by Doubleday, a division of Bantam Doubleday Dell Publishing Group, Inc, New York, NY, 1995.

(3) Seroussi, Karyn, *Unraveling the Mystery of Autism & Pervasive Developmental Disorder: A Mother's Story of Research & Recovery*, Published by Simon & Schuster, New York, NY, 2000, 2002.

(4) Maurice, Catherine, *Let Me Hear Your Voice: A Family's Triumph Over Autism*, A Fawcett Columbine Book, Published by Ballantine Book, a division of Random House, Inc, New York, NY, 1993.

(5) Lovaas, O. Ivar, *Teaching Developmentally Disabled Children: The ME Book*, Published by PRO-ED, Inc, Austin, TX, 1981.

(6) Maurice, p. 226.

(7) Ibid, p. 143.

(8) Ibid, p. 71.

(9) Lovaas, p. 187.

(10) Maurice, p. 69.

(11) Lovaas, p. 24.

(12) Ibid, p. 5.

(13) Ibid, p. 22.

(14) Maurice, p. 87.

(15) *Taber's Cyclopedic Medical Dictionary,* Edition 17, Edited by

Clayton L. Thomas, M.D. M.P.H., Published by F.A. Davis Company, Philadelphia, PA, 1989, p. 177.

(16) Lovaas, pp. 61-69.

(17) Ibid., pp. 71-79.

(18) Lovaas, O. Ivar, *Teaching Individuals with Developmental Delays: Basic Intervention Techniques,* Published by PRO-ED, Inc, Austin, TX, 2002.

(19) Lovaas, *Teaching Developmentally Disabled Children, pp. 64-65.*

(20) Ibid., p. 89.

(21) Ibid., pp. 149-150.

(22) Ibid., pp. 150-152.

(23) Ibid., p. 149.

(24) Maurice, pp. 184-186.

(25) Ibid., pp. 334-335.

(26) Ibid, pp. 214-215.

(27) Ibid., p. 288.

All Scripture references are NKJV